The
BLACKBIRCH ENCYCLOPEDIA
of
Science &
Invention

by Jenny Tesar and Bryan Bunch

VOLUME II
E–K

BLACKBIRCH PRESS, INC.

WOODBRIDGE, CONNECTICUT

How to Use These Books

The Blackbirch Encyclopedia of Science & Invention not only informs readers with entries on key developments, concepts, and people in science, it also presents a "snapshot" background and classification for each topic. To get the most from these books, readers may want to know the purpose of the infographic material that accompanies an entry.

The names and concepts following the idea light bulb 💡 list the people, theories, and discoveries that have contributed significantly to that entry's scientific development. Words or names that appear on the lists in **CAPITAL LETTERS** have a separate entry in the encyclopedia. Likewise, any words or names that appear in **boldface** in the text appear as separate entries in the encyclopedia.

The icons that precede the text of each entry classify it within the scientific world. Here are the fields to which each icon refers.

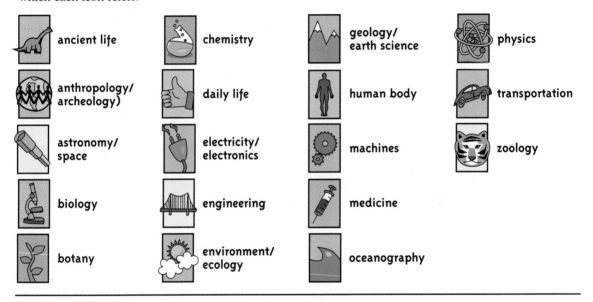

ancient life

chemistry

geology/ earth science

physics

anthropology/ archeology)

daily life

human body

transportation

astronomy/ space

electricity/ electronics

machines

zoology

biology

engineering

medicine

botany

environment/ ecology

oceanography

Published by Blackbirch Press, Inc.
260 Amity Road
Woodbridge, CT 06525
Web site: www.blackbirch.com
e-mail: staff@blackbirch.com

© 2001 Blackbirch Press, Inc.
First Edition

Printed in the United States.

10 9 8 7 6 5 4 3 2 1

Library of Congress Cataloging-in-Publication Data

Tesar, Jenny E.
     The Blackbirch encyclopedia of science and invention / by Jenny Tesar and Bryan Bunch
          p. cm. —
Includes index.
     ISBN 1-56711-576-4 (hardcover: alk. paper)
     1. Science—Encyclopedias, Juvenile. 2. Technology—Encyclopedias, Juvenile. [1. Science—Encyclopedias.
2. Technology—Encyclopedias.] I. Bunch, Bryan H. II. Title

Q121.T47 2001
503—dc21   2001001134

Earle, Sylvia

Oceanographer: made important undersea discoveries
Born: August 30, 1935, Gibbstown, New York

How It Works

The U.S. Tektite Project was named after tektites, glassy products of meteorites found on many ocean bottoms. Underwater missions such as the Tektite Project have had two main objectives. First, occupants of sea-floor chambers can more accurately observe the ocean environment and gather scientific data over an extended period of time. Second, information on the physical and psychological aspects of living underwater is valuable not only to planning permanent seabed outposts but also to the space program.

"On my first visit to the shore, a great wave knocked me off my feet. I've been irresistibly drawn to the ocean ever since," says Earle. She has spent thousands of hours underwater, making discoveries about underwater habitats and identifying many new species.

Earle's first major research, begun in the mid-1950s, focused on algae in the Gulf of Mexico. She has continued this project ever since, and has collected and cataloged more than 20,000 samples. She also discovered undersea sand dunes off the Bahamas.

In 1970, as part of the Tektite Project, Earle and four other women lived for two weeks in a sea-floor chamber on a coral reef in the Virgin Islands. The women moved in and out of the chamber, which had a laboratory and living quarters. In 1979, Earle made the world's deepest solo dive, planting the U.S. flag 1,260 feet (385 m) below the surface on the ocean floor near Hawaii. Untethered, she spent 2 ½ hours exploring the seabed and observing deep-sea life—including glowing fish "that cruised by like miniature ocean liners."

Earle strongly advocates **conservation** and protection of the oceans and their natural resources. "The living ocean drives planetary chemistry, governs climate and weather, and provides the cornerstone of

Sylvia Earle

Notable Quotable

I want to share the exhilaration of discovery and convey a sense of urgency about the need for all of us to use our talents and resources to continue to explore the nature of this extraordinary ocean planet.

—Sylvia Earle

the life-support system for all species on Earth. If the sea is sick, we will feel it. If it dies, we die. Our future and the state of the oceans are one," says Earle.

 **RESOURCES**

- Earle, Sylvia A. *Sea Change: The Message of the Oceans.* New York: Fawcett, 1996.
- Earle, Sylvia A. *Wild Ocean: America's Parks under the Sea.* Washington, DC: National Geographic, 1999.
- MORE ABOUT SYLVIA A. EARLE.
  http://www.literati.net/Earle
- IMPORTANT EVENTS IN OCEAN ENGINEERING HISTORY: UNDERWATER HABITATS.
  http://winnie.fit.edu/swood/History_pg5.html

Earth's Structure

Cavendish (determined Earth's mass) ➤ Daubrée (Earth mass as icon) ➤ Milne (seismograph) ➤ Oldham (measured earthquake waves) ➤ Mohorovicic (boundary line)

People living around the Mediterranean Sea can observe volcanoes such as Vulcan, Stromboli, and Etna, which erupt almost continually. From experience with volcanoes, ancient people concluded that Earth's interior contained fires, though there was no way to know whether Earth was solid rock or hollow.

Scientific information about Earth's internal structure appeared as a by-product of the 1798 experiment of **Henry Cavendish** that determined Earth's mass and suggested that our planet is too dense and heavy to be hollow or even rock. In 1866, based upon the composition of **meteoroids**, Auguste Daubrée [French: 1814–1896] suggested that the heavy substance is iron mixed with nickel. Geologists still think Earth's mass comes from iron.

In 1880, John Milne [English: 1850–1930] invented the modern **seismograph**, which measures earthquake waves. Richard D. Oldham [English: 1858–1936] used the seismograph in 1906 to show that earthquake waves traveling through the center of the Earth are bent by the Earth's core. By 1913 evidence had accumulated that the core is liquid, but closer study of earthquake waves in 1936 showed that only the outer core is liquid. From Earth's center, a solid inner core extends for about 1,110 miles (1,750 km) while the liquid outer core extends another 1,000 miles (1,600 km). From the center of Earth to the surface is 3,963 miles (6,378 km).

In 1909, Andrija Mohorovicic [Croatian: 1857–1936] observed that earthquake waves reveal another boundary line closer to the surface of Earth. This boundary ranges from 50 miles (80 km) deep

Earth's solid inner core

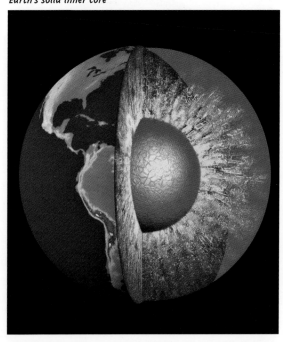

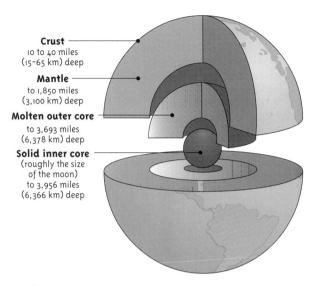

Crust
10 to 40 miles
(15-65 km) deep

Mantle
to 1,850 miles
(3,100 km) deep

Molten outer core
to 3,693 miles
(6,378 km) deep

Solid inner core
(roughly the size
of the moon)
to 3,956 miles
(6,366 km) deep

The structure of Earth

beneath mountains to as little as 3 miles (5 km) below oceans. The region below the Mohorovicic boundary (or Moho) and above the core is called the mantle. The region above the Moho is the crust. The upper part of the crust is mostly solid rock—often called the lithosphere ("ball of rock")—while the lower crust and top of the mantle flow slowly. This partly fluid region is the asthenosphere ("ball of weakness"). According to **plate tectonics**, parts of the lithosphere float on the asthenosphere.

 RESOURCES

• Downs, Sandra. *Earth's Hidden Treasures*. New York: Twenty-First Century, 1999. (JUV/YA)

• Gallant, Roy A. and Christopher J. Schuberth. *Earth: The Making of a Planet*. Tarrytown, NY: Marshall Cavendish, 1998.

• MORE ABOUT EARTH'S STRUCTURE.

http://www.geologyone.com/esa/geopro/platec2/platec2.html

http://www.seismo.unr.edu/ftp/pub/louie/class/100/interior.html

Eastman, George

Inventor: improved cameras and film
Born: July 12, 1854, Waterville, New York
Died: March 14, 1932, Rochester, New York

 When Eastman began taking pictures in the 1870s, "My layout had in it a camera about the size of a soap box, a tripod which was strong and heavy enough to support a bungalow, a big plate holder, a dark tent, a nitrate bath, and a container for water." He forgot to mention the heavy glass plates that had to be coated with an emulsion and, while still wet, put in the camera, exposed to light, and almost immediately processed. No wonder only a few amateurs and professionals took pictures!

George Eastman

The process first used by Eastman was called wet-plate **photography**. In 1879, Eastman patented a process to make dry photographic plates. But he wanted to make photography available to everyone—"to make the camera as convenient as the pencil."

During the following years, Eastman introduced flexible film and, in 1888, the Kodak box camera ("Kodak" is a word he invented). He organized his business as the Eastman Kodak Company and in 1900 introduced the Brownie camera, which was small and simple enough to be used by children. Thanks to Eastman, photography became a popular hobby among people of all ages.

 RESOURCES

• Brayer, Elizabeth. *George Eastman: A Biography*. Baltimore: John Hopkins, 1996.
• MORE ABOUT GEORGE EASTMAN.
  http://www.kodak.com/aboutKodak/kodakHistory/eastman.shtml

Ecology

 THEOPHRASTUS (described communities of organisms) ➤ LINNAEUS/DARWIN/WALLACE (plant and animal observation) ➤ Volterra/Lotka (predator-prey population models) ➤ Gause (ecological niches) ➤ Tansley (ecosystems)

 Ecology—the study of the interactions of organisms with their environments—is a relatively young science. It is, however, based on work done over more than 2,000 years. Around 370 B.C.E., **Theophrastus** described relationships within communities of organisms. In the 18th and 19th centuries explorers and naturalists such as **Carolus Linnaeus**, **Charles Darwin**, and **Alfred Russel Wallace** traveled widely, kept detailed notes of their observations of plants and animals, and collected numerous specimens. Early work in **physiology** and **evolution** also helped lay the foundations of ecology. Ernst Haeckel [German: 1834–1919] coined the word "ecology" and gave its first definition in 1866.

An ecological community includes both living (deer) and non-living (air) factors.

During the early part of the 20th century, botanists focused on plant communities—that is, populations that live together in specific areas. Some botanists studied the composition, structure, and distribution of plant communities while others studied succession (how communities change and gradually replace one another). Animal communities were studied separately until it became apparent that the inter-relationships of plants and animals are a critical aspect of ecology.

Lions are important predators in the African savannah ecosystem.

Meanwhile, other scientists explored the factors that determine population size and growth. In the 1920s Vito Volterra [Italian: 1860–1940] and Alfred Lotka [American: 1880–1949] created mathematical models to describe changes in predator-prey populations and how competition between species affects populations. The concepts of **food pyramids and chains** also were developed in the 1920s, as was the idea of the ecological niche (the position and interactions of a species within its community). Georgii F. Gause [Russian: 1910–1986], who studied competition and predation among protozoans, used Volterra's models to show that, "if two or more species live in stable association, they must possess different ecological niches."

Modern ecology is based on the concept of ecosystems, a term coined in 1935 by Arthur Tansley [English: 1871–1955], who noted that, "We cannot separate [organisms] from their specific environment, with which they form one physical system." An ecosystem consists of a community of organisms and the physical environment in which they live.

FAMOUS FIRST

In a 1917 article on thrashers, a common bird in California's chaparral communities, Joseph Grinnell [American: 1877–1939] correctly proposed that no two species can have exactly the same niche in the same community. He also said that organisms evolve to fill niches.

 **RESOURCES**

• Bowler, Peter J. *The Earth Encompassed: A History of the Environmental Sciences*. New York: W.W. Norton, 2000.

• BIOME DOME.
  http://www.dgl.salem.mass.edu/profs/young/students/bio-biome/biomedom.htm

Edgerton, Harold E.

Engineer: invented ultra-high-speed and stop-action photography
Born: April 6, 1903, Fremont, Nebraska
Died: January 4, 1990, Cambridge, Massachusetts

A falling drop of milk. A tennis racket hitting a ball. A bullet piercing an apple. These actions happen too fast for the human eye to see, but Edgerton figured out how to capture them in a fascinating series of photographs.

In the late 1920s, Edgerton began working with a stroboscope, a device that generates brief flashes of light at a rapid rate. When a single flash illuminates a moving object, the object appears to be stopped completely. When a series of flashes is used, the object appears to move in jerks, creating a slow-motion effect. Edgerton synchronized strobe flashes with the movement of an object. Then he photographed the object using a camera with its shutter open, thereby capturing the object in a series of locations. The technique soon found many uses. For example, scientists used it to record and analyze air currents.

During World War II, Edgerton designed a strobe device for nighttime aerial photography of enemy targets. In addition, Edgerton's work led to the electronic flash used in modern photography.

Edgerton also was interested in underwater exploration, traveling with **Jacques-Yves Cousteau** and other oceanographers. He improved underwater cameras so they could withstand water pressure and

Edgerton's stroboscopic photos capture actions that happen too rapidly for the human eye to see.

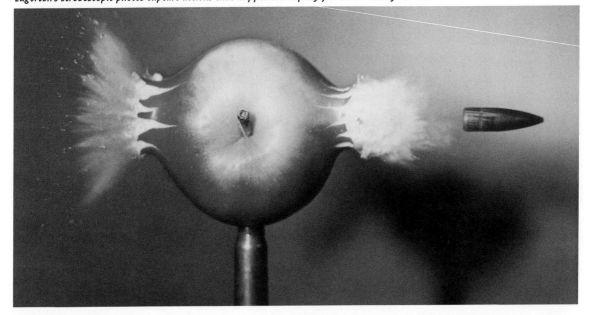

developed side-scan sonar equipment, which helped scientists visualize the shape of objects on the ocean floor.

 **RESOURCES**

- Edgerton, Harold E. *Exploring the Art and Science of Stopping Time: A CD-ROM Based on the Life and Work of Harold E. Edgerton.* Cambridge, MA: MIT, 1999.

- SEEING THE UNSEEN: DR. HAROLD E. EDGERTON AND THE WONDERS OF STROBE ALLEY.

  http://www.cmp.ucr.edu/exhibitions/
  edgerton/edgerton.html

- SIMPLIFIED STROBOSCOPIC SYSTEM FOR MOTION PATTERN PHOTOGRAPHY.

  http://www.rit.edu/andpph/
  text-stroboscope.html

Edison, Thomas Alva

Inventor: created phonograph, incandescent light bulb, motion picture machine
Born: February 11, 1847, Milan, Ohio
Died: October 18, 1931, West Orange, New Jersey

 "I find out what the world needs, then I go ahead and try to invent it," Edison once said.

Notable Quotable

All you need to be an inventor is a good imagination and a pile of junk.

My business is thinking.

Results? Why, man, I have gotten lots of results! If I find 10,000 ways something won't work, I haven't failed. I am not discouraged, because every wrong attempt discarded is another step forward. Just because something doesn't do what you planned it to do doesn't mean it's useless.

—Thomas Alva Edison

Thomas Alva Edison

He was the most prolific inventor of all time, receiving 1,093 patents in the United States alone and laying the groundwork for many technological innovations of the 20th century.

Edison presented his first major invention, a machine to record votes, in 1868. He then contributed to the development of the **telegraph** and **telephone**. In 1877 he invented the phonograph, introducing the idea of **sound recording**. His first phonograph had a steel needle that transferred sounds to a waxed cylinder wrapped in tin foil. The sounds were of poor quality and Edison initially viewed the phonograph as "a mere toy, which has no commercial value." Later, he considered it his favorite among all his inventions.

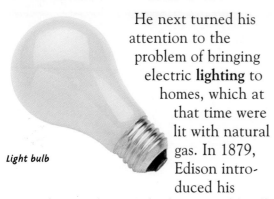

Light bulb

He next turned his attention to the problem of bringing electric **lighting** to homes, which at that time were lit with natural gas. In 1879, Edison introduced his incandescent lamp (which we would call a light bulb), which had a carbon filament sealed in a glass globe containing a partial vacuum. Electric current heated the filament to a brilliant glow (incandescence) and, because of the absence of oxygen, the filament did not melt or burn out. Meanwhile, Edison planned an electricity distribution system—with dynamos, insulated underground cables, meters for measuring consumption, outlets, and switches—to carry electricity to houses.

Edison also discovered that he could cause an electric current to flow between his lamp's filament and a separate electrode

Early phonograph

inside the glass globe. This came to be called the Edison effect and led to development by **John Ambrose Fleming** and others of vacuum tubes, used in early **radios, computers**, and other electronic equipment.

In 1891, Edison patented the first machine to produce **motion pictures**. Called the kinetoscope, it used 35-millimeter film and produced 46 pictures per second. In 1903 he produced one of the first movies, *The Great Train Robbery*.

Yet another major invention, Edison's dry storage battery, came in 1904. This battery gave electrical equipment its own source of power and is the basis of **batteries** now used in gasoline-powered vehicles and many other devices.

 RESOURCES

- Adair, Gene. *Thomas Alva Edison: Inventing the Electric Age.* New York: Oxford, 1997. (JUV/YA)
- Israel, Paul. *Edison: A Life of Invention.* New York: John Wiley, 1998.
- Recording Technology History.
  http://history.acusd.edu/gen/recording/notes.html
- More about Thomas Alva Edison.
  http://edison.rutgers.edu/
  http://www.thomasedison.com/

Ehrlich, Paul

Bacteriologist: helped found immunology and chemotherapy
Born: March 14, 1854, Strehlen, Silesia (now Strzelin, Poland)
Died: August 20, 1915, Bad Homburg, Germany

 Ehrlich did pioneering work in three fields: hematology (the study of blood), immunology (the study of organisms' ability to resist disease), and chemotherapy (the use of chemicals to fight

made one of the earliest attempts to explain **immunity**, saying that body cells produce special "side-chains" to attack invading bacteria and provide future defense against disease.

Ehrlich believed that some chemicals might be "magic bullets" that attack disease organisms without harming human cells. He synthesized a compound he called Salvarsan and in 1910 successfully used it to cure syphilis. He named this new technique chemotherapy.

 RESOURCES

• BIOGRAPHY OF PAUL EHRLICH.

http://www.nobel.se/laureates/
medicine-1908-2-bio.html

Einstein, Albert

Physicist: created relativity theory
Born: March 14, 1879, Ulm, Germany
Died: April 18, 1955, Princeton, New Jersey

 Einstein was the most famous 20th-century scientist, so well known that "Einstein" is popularly used to mean "genius." This fame is appropriate, for he was the most influential physicist of his day. His contributions began in

Paul Ehrlich

disease). While still a university student, he began using aniline dyes to stain cells and structures within cells, making them easier to see. In this manner, he discovered the different kinds of white blood cells.

In 1890, Ehrlich joined **Robert Koch**'s Institute for Infectious Diseases, where he established the proper dosages for **Emil von Behring**'s diphtheria antitoxin. He

NOBEL PRIZE 1908

The Nobel Prize in physiology or medicine was awarded to Ehrlich and Elie Metchnikoff [Russian: 1845–1916] for their work on immunity. Metchnikoff discovered how white blood cells help fight infection.

FAMOUS FIRST

Einstein was the first to establish that molecules exist, that waves can behave as particles, that energy can change into matter and matter into energy, that time moves at different speeds in different locations, and that nothing can travel faster than the speed of light. He accomplished this all during one year—1905.

1905 with three major results, any one of which would have assured him a place in the history of science.

Before Einstein, chemists and physicists had concluded that matter was made from small particles in motion—atoms and molecules. But no proof that this was true existed. One of Einstein's 1905 proofs analyzed movements of microscopic particles in solution. Since 1827, when **Robert Brown** first saw pollen particles dancing about, this Brownian motion had been unexplained. Einstein showed that the movements resulted from pushes by tiny molecules, establishing that molecules exist, even though unseen.

Albert Einstein

NOBEL PRIZE 1921

Einstein's Nobel Prize in physics was for his discovery that light knocks electrons out of metals as if light consists of particles, not waves,

Another 1905 paper explained that **light**—viewed at that time as composed only of waves—behaves like a particle when knocking electrons out of metal (a **photoelectric phenomenon** known as the photoelectric effect). That something can be both a particle and a wave became the foundation of **quantum theory**.

Einstein's third advance of 1905 was his theory linking time to space, and energy to matter—the theory of special relativity. It led to the famous equation $E = mc^2$, showing matter is a form of energy.

From 1907 to 1915 Einstein developed the theory of general relativity, the foundation of cosmology (the science of the **universe** as a whole). General relativity describes how gravity interacts with space and implies both that the universe must expand and that black holes exist. In

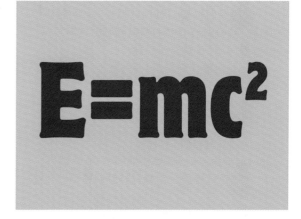

1919 astronomers tested the effects of gravity on light, and found general relativity more accurate than the gravitational theory of **Isaac Newton**. This led to Einstein's worldwide fame.

Einstein's later years were marked with failure to achieve difficult goals, but even in failure he made fundamental contributions. In 1935 he concentrated on showing that **subatomic particles** must follow the same rules of cause and effect as larger objects do. Although Einstein was wrong, his analysis led to an important development in the 1990s called teleportation, in which information appears to travel instantly from one subatomic particle to another (Einstein called the idea "spooky action at a distance"). Einstein also attempted, unsuccessfully, to unify electromagnetism and gravity into a single theory.

 RESOURCES

- Bernstein, Jeremy. *Albert Einstein and the Frontiers of Physics.* New York: Oxford Children's, 1997. (JUV/YA)
- Clark, Ronald W. *Einstein: The Life and Times.* New York: Avon, 1984.
- Goldenstern, Joyce. *Albert Einstein: Physicist and Genius* (Great Minds of Science). Berkeley Heights, NJ: Enslow, 1995. (JUV/YA)
- ALBERT EINSTEIN.
  http://www.westegg.com/einstein

Einthoven, Willem

Physiologist: made first reliable electrocardiograph
Born: May 21, 1860, Samarang, Java
Died: September 28, 1927, Amsterdam, Netherlands

 In 1842, Carlo Matteucci [Italian: 1811–1868] showed that an electric current accompanies each heartbeat.

Willem Einthoven

This led to efforts to design an instrument that could record electrocardiograms (tracings of the changes in a heart's electrical activity). The most commonly used devices during the late 1800s, called capillary electrometers, were not sensitive and had other drawbacks.

Around 1901, Einthoven designed the first reliable electrocardiograph. Called a string galvanometer, it consisted of a silver-coated quartz wire (string) suspended in a magnetic field. When electric current created naturally by contracting heart muscle passed through the wire, the wire was deflected slightly;

NOBEL PRIZE 1924
Einthoven received the Nobel Prize in physiology or medicine for developing the string galvanometer.

this movement was recorded on a photographic plate.

Einthoven published the first electrocardiogram recorded on a string galvanometer in 1902. In 1905 he began sending electrocardiograms via telephone from a hospital to his laboratory 0.9 mile (1.5 km) away. Einthoven continued to improve his string galvanometer, and showed that it could detect and diagnose heart abnormalities, thereby revolutionizing the study of heart disease.

RESOURCES
- Biography of Willem Einthoven.
  http://www.nobel.se/medicine/laureates/1924/einthoven-bio.html
- Brief History of Electrocardiography.
  http://homepages.enterprise.net/djenkins/ecghist.html

Above: *Large relay stations help distribute electric power.*
Below: *Machines such as this mixer use electric power.*

Electric Power

Henry/Faraday (first electric motors) ➤
Edison/Swan (electric-powered lamps, coal-powered generators) ➤ Tesla (high-voltage AC current)

In 1831, **Joseph Henry** built the first electric motor, capturing the force between magnets and current electricity to generate motion. **Michael Faraday** also built electric motors in that year. Both recognized that their motors could also work backward, turning motion into electricity. For the next 35 years, many inventors built versions of reverse motors, called electric generators, adding various improvements. Practical generators existed by 1867. A steam engine or a water-powered turbine supplied the motion.

Electric power in the 1870s could be generated, but there was little use for it at

the time. In 1879, however, **Thomas Alva Edison** and Joseph Swan [English: 1828–1914] each invented practical electric-powered lamps. In 1882, Edison built a plant using coal-powered generators in New York City, and the first water-powered generator began operations in Appleton, Wisconsin. Soon most communities were wired for power and hundreds of applications for electricity were invented.

The first power generated was direct current (DC), which moves in one direction only and weakens if it must travel any distance. Alternating current (AC) changes direction 60 times a second. In 1891, **Nikola Tesla** developed a way to produce high-voltage AC current that can travel long distances over power lines. All power today is delivered as AC. If DC is needed, a transformer is used.

  RESOURCES

• Kaiser, Joe. *Electrical Power: Motors, Controls, Generators, Transformers*. Tinley Park, IL: Goodheart-Willcox, 1998.

• Parker, Steve. *Eyewitness: Electricity*. New York, NY: DK, 2000. (JUV/YA)

• MORE ABOUT ELECTRIC POWER.
  http://www.iclei.org/efacts/

Electrolysis

VOLTA (invented batteries) ➤ DAVY (more powerful battery) ➤ FARADAY (laws of electrolysis)

Electrolysis means "electrically unbinding," an appropriate description of this chemical reaction triggered by electricity. Electrolysis also means destruction of animal tissues by electricity, referring most often to a method used to remove hair.

 How It Works

A metal rod, called a pole, is supplied with current and inserted into a liquid along with another pole. Electrolysis requires a liquid containing ions, charged parts of molecules. Positive ions move to the negative pole, where they acquire electrons. In the case of water the positive ion is H^+, which combines with its mates to release hydrogen (H_2) at the negative pole. The negative ion is OH. Four OH^- ions combine at the positive pole to form two H_2O molecules and to release one O_2 molecule.

In 1800, William Nicholson [English: 1753–1815] learned that **Alessandro Volta** had invented batteries that produce current electricity. Nicholson built a battery which he used to break water into hydrogen and oxygen, the first chemical reaction induced by current electricity. **Humphry Davy** developed a more powerful battery that he used to discover several new elements, starting with potassium and sodium in 1807. Davy's assistant, **Michael Faraday**, continued the work with electrolysis. In 1832, Faraday stated laws that connect amount of current, mass, atomic weight, and the way that chemicals can combine, known as valence. Faraday's laws of electrolysis were partly explained in 1887 by theories of Svante Arrhenius [Swedish: 1859–1927], since refined by electrochemists.

 **RESOURCES**

• MORE ABOUT ELECTROLYSIS.
  http://edie.cprost.sfu.ca/rhlogan/electrol.html

Electronics

FARADAY (light from electric current through gas)
➤ **PLÜCKER** (better vacuum) ➤ **THOMSON** (identified electrons) ➤ **EDISON** (metal filament in light bulb)
➤ **FLEMING** (Edison effect, vacuum tube or diode) ➤
DE FOREST (triode) ➤ **BARDEEN/BRATTAIN** (transistor)
➤ **KILBY/NOYCE** (silicon chips)

Electronic devices, such as vacuum tubes or **transistors**, operate because of the movement of electrons, while electric devices, such as lamps and motors, employ electric fields that move through conductors. Electrons—**subatomic particles** of negative charge—pass through a vacuum in electronic devices or overcome thin barriers.

Electronics began when **Michael Faraday** tried to pass an electric current through a low-pressure gas in a glass tube, which caused the gas to emit light. Julius Plücker [German: 1801–1868] in 1858 found that improving the vacuum causes a spot on the glass to glow instead of the gas itself. By 1869, scientists recognized that an

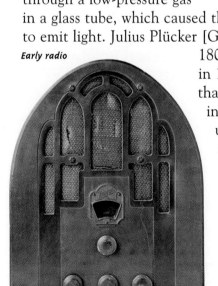

A microprocessor

Early radio

invisible ray, soon identified as a stream of charged particles, induces the glow. This stream was named a cathode ray by Eugen Goldstein [German: 1850–1930] in 1876. In 1897, **J.J. Thomson** measured the mass of the tiny particles in the stream, identifying them as electrons. Thus, the cathode-ray tube, used in television and computer monitors, was the first electronic device.

In 1883, **Thomas Alva Edison** discovered that the heated metal filament in a light bulb produces a flow of electricity that can be picked up by a nearby conductor in the bulb. **John Ambrose Fleming** worked with Edison at the time and later investigated this Edison effect. After the electron was discovered, Fleming recognized that a hot filament or plate in a vacuum tube gives off electrons that travel to a cold plate in the same tube. In 1904, Fleming used the Edison effect to invent the second electronic device, which he called a valve (since electricity flows though it in one direction only). Americans call the same device a vacuum tube, and electrical engineers refer to it as a diode ("two electrodes"). In 1907, **Lee De Forest** added a third electrode to a diode and created the triode, which controls the amount of current flowing through the tube. The diode and triode made radio practical, while variations on these vacuum tubes became the basis of many electronic devices, including early computers.

How It Works

Metals contain electrons not bound to particular atoms. As a metal is heated, these electrons gain speed and some fly off the surface. A nearby positively charged conductor attracts these electrons, setting up a current. A vacuum permits electrons to move freely from the hot metal to the nearby conductor.

 RESOURCES

- Bridgman, Roger. *Eyewitness: Electronics.* New York: DK, 2000. (JUV/YA)
- Dummer, G.W.A. and E. Davies. *Electronic Inventions and Discoveries: Electronics from Its Earliest Beginnings to the Present Day.* London: Institute of Physics, 1997.
- MORE ABOUT ELECTRONICS.

  http://www.ee.umd.edu/taylor/Electrons.htm

  http://www.etedeschi.ndirect.co.uk/museum/concise.history.htm

Certain crystals, which conduct electricity in one direction only, were often used in early radio instead of diodes. In 1947, **John Bardeen** and Walter H. Brattain [American: 1902–1987], created the first transistor, an improved version of such a crystal. By the 1950s, transistors were replacing vacuum tubes. In 1958, Jack Kilby [American: 1923–] and Robert Noyce [American: 1927–1990] independently developed silicon chips that contain many transistors working together. These became the workhorses of electronics, especially in **computers**. Computer chips are also used to control operations in automobiles, telephones, ovens, and many other common devices.

Several semiconductors, such as selenium, can free electrons using the energy of light (first observed in 1861). Photoelectric cells of various types are also electronic devices, as are the key elements in copying machines.

Elevators and Escalators

 The dividing line between an elevator and a platform lifted with a rope over a beam or pulley is rather hazy.

An escalator

Various lifting devices, usually called "hoists" and operated by hand, animal power, or steam were used for hundreds of years. The modern elevator, or lift, originated with **Elisha Graves Otis** in 1852. The Otis elevator is often credited with making skyscrapers possible. The first passenger elevators, installed in buildings starting in 1857, were steam powered, but in the 1880s elevators began to use electric motors.

A moving stairway is an escalator, originally a trade name combining a French word for climbing with "elevator." It was invented in 1892 by Jesse Wilford Reno [American: 1861–1947]. People were somewhat afraid of it at first. In 1911, a British firm hired a one-legged man to ride up and down one of the first escalators in London to show its safety.

 RESOURCES

- Barner, Bob. *Elevator Escalator Book: A Transportation Fact Book.* New York: Doubleday, 1990. (JUV/YA)
- ESCALATOR HISTORY.
  http://www.covent-garden.co.uk/Histories/escalators.html

Elion, Gertrude

Organic chemist: developed new medicines
Born: January 23, 1918, New York, New York
Died: February 21, 1999, Chapel Hill, North Carolina

  As a young woman, Elion was eager to become a medical researcher, but it wasn't until World War II pulled men from their jobs that Elion was able to get work in a laboratory, though not in research. Finally in 1944 she was hired by George H. Hitching [American: 1905–1998] at Wellcome Research

Gertrude Elion

Laboratories. For the next 40 years the two collaborated on developing new drugs.

Instead of using the trial-and-error approach taken by most drug developers, Elion and Hitching studied the biochemical characteristics of normal and cancerous cells, and of bacteria, viruses, and other pathogens (disease-causing organisms). They used this knowledge to create drugs that could kill or inhibit a specific

Notable Quotable

When we began to see the results of our efforts in the form of new drugs which filled real medical needs and benefited patients in very visible ways, our feeling of reward was immeasurable.

—Gertrude Elion

NOBEL PRIZE 1988

Elion and Hitching shared the Nobel Prize in physiology or medicine with James W. Black [British: 1924–] "for their discoveries of important principles for drug treatment."

pathogen without harming the patient's normal cells. Elion developed drugs to combat leukemia, gout, malaria, and herpes. In 1957 she created the first immunosup-

FAMOUS FIRST

Elion helped oversee development of azidothymidine (AZT), the first drug approved by the U.S. Food & Drug Administration (in 1987) to fight the virus that causes AIDS.

pressant, a drug that suppresses the immune system and thereby helps prevent rejection of **organ transplants**.

 RESOURCES

- AUTOBIOGRAPHY OF GERTRUDE B. ELION.
- http://www.nobel.se/medicine/ laureates/1988/elion-autobio.html
- OBITUARY FOR GERTRUDE ELION.
  http://www.wellesley.edu/Chemistry/ chem227/news/obit-elion.html

Endeavour Expedition

Began: August 26, 1768
Ended: July 12, 1771

 Astronomers in the 1700s lacked data needed to calculate the size of the solar system from **Isaac Newton**'s laws. The time it takes Venus to cross (transit) the face of the Sun, observed from several locations, could provide the answer. One transit in 1761 was obscured by bad weather. Another transit would occur in 1769, but none after for over a century. Several expeditions to observe the 1769 transit were mounted. The English Royal Society, a scientific organization, financed one voyage to the South Pacific.

Captain James Cook [English: 1728–1779] headed the Royal Society expedition and Joseph Banks [English: 1743–1820], a botanist, was the chief scientist. Cook chose a ship designed to carry coal in the North Sea, renamed the *Endeavour*. It proved sturdy even after being grounded on the Great Barrier Reef

James Cook led the Endeavor Expedition

CAPTAIN JAMES COOK F.R.S.

off Australia. Most of the crew of 94 also survived the voyage, in part because Cook forced them to eat sauerkraut, high in vitamin C, daily to avoid the common shipboard disease scurvy.

Successful observation of the transit became only a part of the scientific harvest. Cook, an excellent navigator and surveyor, charted both islands of New Zealand, explored the east coast of Australia, and discovered unknown islands. Cook also made anthropological notes on native cultures. Banks and his team discovered many new plants and animals, bringing back seeds, skins, and dramatic watercolor pictures.

Cook made two later voyages to the Pacific, from the southern ice floes surrounding Antarctica to their northern counterparts off Alaska, discovering the Hawaiian Islands in between.

 **RESOURCES**

- Hough, Richard. *Captain James Cook: A Biography*. Bridgewater, NJ: Replica, 1998.
- Morriss, Roger. *Captain Cook & His Exploration of the Pacific*. New York: Barrons Juveniles, 1998. (JUV/YA)
- MORE ABOUT CAPTAIN COOK AND ENDEAVOUR.
  http://www.geocities.com/Athens/Delphi/5600/cookbook.htm
  http://www.gold.ac.uk/world/endeavour/maritime.html

Enders, John Franklin

Virologist: grew polio virus in test tubes
Born: February 10, 1897, West Hartford, Connecticut
Died: September 8, 1985, Waterford, Connecticut

 Viruses are different from bacteria and other organisms. They can grow and reproduce only in living cells. By

John Franklin Enders

1925 it had been proven that some viruses can grow in **tissue cultures**—that is, in test tubes containing a nutrient substance and fragments of plant or animal tissue. But all efforts to grow polio viruses in tissue cultures were unsuccessful. These viruses could only be grown in nerve tissue in living animals, which was expensive, time-consuming, and yielded only small samples for study.

NOBEL PRIZE 1954

Enders, Robbins, and Weller shared the Nobel Prize in physiology or medicine for their discovery that the polio virus can be grown in cultures of various types of tissues.

In 1948, Enders and his colleagues Frederick Robbins [American: 1916–] and Thomas Weller [American: 1915–] developed an improved technique for culturing viruses. They tried growing polio viruses in a culture of human embryonic tissue and were successful in their very first attempts. They also succeeded in growing polio viruses in skin, muscle, intestine, and other tissue. Equally important, they were able to isolate the viruses from the tissue cultures. This enabled scientists to grow polio viruses in large quantities, leading to development of the first polio vaccine by **Jonas Edward Salk.**

 RESOURCES

• MORE ABOUT JOHN FRANKLIN ENDERS.

  http://www.nobel.se/medicine/laureates/
  1954/enders-bio.html

  http://www.nobel.se/medicine/laureates/
  1954/press.html

Engelbart, Douglas

Engineer: invented the computer mouse
Born: January 30, 1925, Portland, Oregon

 In the early 1960s several devices were available to enter information into **computers,** including keyboards, light pens, and joysticks. None of these easily controlled what happened on the computer screen. Engelbart wanted

A computer mouse

something that was more efficient yet easy to use. He built the mouse—a palm-sized box with one or more control buttons on top; moving the mouse across a tabletop moves a pointer on the computer screen. It can be used to choose commands from menus, move objects on the screen, and draw pictures onscreen.

YEARBOOK: 1967

• Engelbart files his patent application for the computer mouse.

• Mammography (X-ray examination) for early detection of breast cancer is introduced.

• **Jocelyn Bell Burnell** discovers the first pulsar.

Engelbart also contributed to development of many other characteristics of modern computing, including the concept of having several programs running at the same time, video teleconferencing, e-mail, and the **Internet.**

 RESOURCES

• MORE ABOUT DOUGLAS ENGELBART.

  http://www.public.iastate.edu/rjsalvad/
  engelbart.html

  http://www.isocanda.org/pioneros/Engelbart/
  de.htm

  http://www.invent.org/book/book-text/
  engelbart.html

ENIAC

ENIAC, one of the first electronic **computers,** is considered by many people to have been the most influential of the early machines. It showed that science and industry could benefit from using computers, and led to the birth of the computer industry. It was started during World War II, when people used mechanical calculators to develop firing tables. Firing tables, which consist of thousands of calculations concerning the trajectory (path) a cannon shell or other projectile will take, are used by artillery crews to accurately aim weapons. John W. Mauchly [American: 1907–1980] and J. Presper Eckert [American: 1919–1995] at the University of Pennsylvania proposed a high-speed digital computer to handle the calculations. In 1943, the U.S. Army awarded a contract to build the machine, which was called the Electronic Numerical Integrator and Computer, or ENIAC.

ENIAC weighed 30 tons and filled 1,800 square feet of space. It had over 100,000 electronic components, including 17,468 vacuum tubes.

A skilled person needed about 20 hours to compute a 60-second trajectory. ENIAC needed only 30 seconds. But by the time ENIAC was finished in late 1945, World War II was over. Instead of firing tables, the military was studying nuclear weapons. ENIAC's first application was to perform calculations of a proposed design for a hydrogen bomb.

RESOURCES

- McCartney, Scott. *ENIAC: The Triumphs and Tragedies of the World's First Computer.* New York: Walker, 1999.
- ENIAC VIRTUAL MUSEUM.
  http://www.seas.upenn.edu/museum/directory.html

Entropy

Clausius (second law of thermodynamics) ➤ **Maxwell/Boltzmann** (mathematical approach to heat and temperature in gases) ➤ **Shannon** (entropy as a measure of any kind of disorder)

Heat cannot by itself move from a region of low temperature to one of high temperature. This principle, known as the second law of thermodynamics, was stated clearly by Rudolph Clausius [German: 1822–1888] in 1850. Several other physicists independently recognized similar ideas about that time. In 1865, Clausius introduced the word "entropy"—defined as the ratio of change in amount of heat to temperature—to give the law a mathematical basis. Using entropy (Greek for "transformation"), the second law becomes, "In a closed system, entropy always increases."

Over time, scientists have expanded the definition of entropy—all versions are true, but each new one encompasses and surpasses the previous ones. **James Clerk Maxwell** and Ludwig Boltzmann [Austrian: 1844–1906] developed a mathematical approach to heat and

The change in heat causes the transformation of water from one state to another.

temperature in gases, which enabled Boltzmann in 1877 to define entropy in terms of probability. Boltzmann showed that entropy is a measure of disorder; for example, when a liquid freezes, its molecules form highly ordered crystals, a lower entropy state.

Entropy is unusual in having only one natural direction—up. Entropy of the whole universe rises over time. Other physical quantities, such as energy, usually stay the same. Most physical interactions can be reversed, but not entropy. Consequently, entropy is sometimes said to determine the direction of time. All bodies in the universe will someday be the same temperature, a condition that has been named "the heat death of the universe."

In 1948, Claude Shannon [American: 1916–] recognized that in a mathematical theory of information and codes, the concept of entropy is the same as the amount of uncertainty in a message. Since then, entropy has been used as a measure of any kind of disorder.

RESOURCES

• Berry, R. Stephen. *Understanding Energy: Energy, Entropy and Thermodynamics for Every Man.* River Edge, NJ: World Scientific, 1991.

• MORE ABOUT ENTROPY.

  http://www.math.washington.edu/hillman/entropy.html

Enzymes

Enzymes are complex proteins, found in every living organism, that act as catalysts. Like all catalysts they speed up chemical reactions without being destroyed or permanently changed during the reactions. A single cell may contain thousands of different enzymes, each designed to catalyze one or a few reactions.

Interest in brewing beer led to the discovery of enzymes. In 1833, Anselme Payen [French: 1795–1871] and Jean Persoz [French: 1806–1868] partly isolated amylase, the agent that breaks down starch to sugar during **fermentation** of beer. Two years later Jöns Berzelius [Swedish: 1779–1848] introduced the concept of

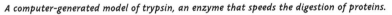

A computer-generated model of trypsin, an enzyme that speeds the digestion of proteins.

catalysis, using amylase as an example.

At first, amylase and similar substances discovered during the following decades

> ## FAMOUS FIRST
> In 1969, using an automated procedure he had developed several years earlier, R. Bruce Merrifield [American: 1921–] made the first synthetic enzyme, a copy of ribonuclease.

were called "ferments" but this term was replaced by "enzymes," suggested by Wilhelm Kuhne [German: 1837–1900] in 1867. **Louis Pasteur** proved that fermentation is catalyzed by enzymes and argued that the enzymes must contain living material. Others, notably Justus von Liebig [German: 1803–1873], said that enzymes are nonliving substances produced by living cells. The dispute was settled in the 1890s by Eduard Buchner [German: 1860–1917], who produced a cell-free juice containing active enzymes.

The myriad roles of enzymes in **metabolism** became clear during the 20th century, with work by **Hans Krebs** and others. In 1926, James Sumner [American: 1887–1955] crystallized an enzyme for the first time and demonstrated that enzymes are proteins. In the 1940s George Beadle [American: 1903–1989] and Edward Tatum [American: 1909–1975] demonstrated that synthesis of each

enzyme is controlled by a specific gene. If a **mutation** occurs in the gene, the enzyme is changed, preventing it from doing its job properly.

 RESOURCES

- INDUSTRIAL ENZYMES.
  http://www.novozymes.com/cgi-bin/ bvisapi.dll/discover/ discover.jsp?cid=-9281&id=13226

Epidemiology

JENNER (smallpox control via inoculation) ➤ Snow (cholera transmission by contaminated water) ➤ KOCH and others (microorganisms cause disease) ➤ vaccines/pesticides/sanitation

The science of epidemiology studies how **disease** spreads through a group of people—or even across a continent or around the world—and how specific diseases can be controlled. An early—and often unsuccessful—attempt to control a spreading disease was the quarantine, a waiting period of 40 days before entering a city, used in 14th-century Europe in hopes of stopping transmission of plague.

The science developed in the 1800s following **Edward Jenner's** demonstration that the spread of smallpox can be limited by inoculation. In 1854, John Snow [English: 1813–1858] showed that cholera is transmitted by contaminated water; through careful observation he linked a cholera epidemic in London with certain community pumps and ended the epidemic by ordering the removal of pump handles, thereby making the pumps unusable.

Discoveries in the second half of the 1800s by **Robert Koch** and others that microorganisms cause disease hastened

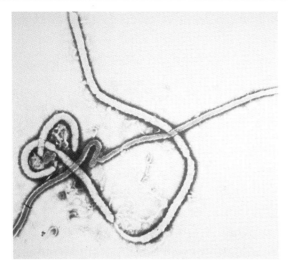

Ebola virus

diseases—recently identified diseases such as AIDS, Ebola, and hantavirus.
See also immunity.

 **RESOURCES**

• Hoff, Brent H., and Carter Smith III. *Mapping Epidemics: A Historical Atlas of Disease.* Danbury, CT: Franklin Watts, 2000. (JUV/YA)

• Epidemic! The World of Infectious Disease.
  http://www.amnh.org/exhibitions/epidemic/

• John Snow: A Historical Giant in Epidemiology.
  http://www.ph.ucla.edu/epi/snow.html

understanding of how many diseases spread. Control measures could then be instituted in following years: **vaccines** were developed against many infectious diseases, **pesticides** were introduced to rid areas of disease-carrying mosquitoes, **sanitation** laws were strengthened, smoking curbs were enacted to prevent lung cancer, and so on.

At the beginning of the 21st century, an important focus of epidemiology is emerging

Eratosthenes

Mathematician and astronomer: measured diameter of Earth
Born: 276 B.C.E., Cyrene (now Libya)
Died: 194 B.C.E., Alexandria, Egypt

 Eratosthenes was the first person known to have calculated Earth's diameter. He observed a difference in how the Sun's rays fell at two towns in Egypt: Syene (now Aswan), where at noon the sun was directly overhead, and Alexandria, about 500 miles (800 km)

When the sun was directly over Syene (S), at Alexandria (A) its light fell at an angle (y) of about 7°. Eratosthenes used this and the distance from Syene to Alexandria (L) to calculate Earth's radius (R)—the distance between the surface and Earth's center (C).

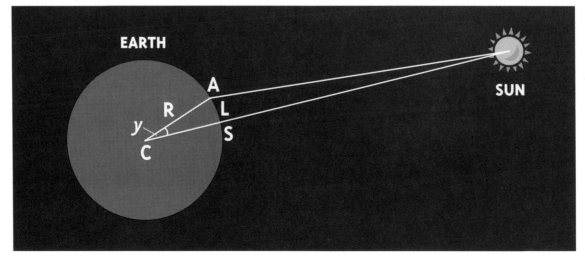

north of Syene, where at noon on the same day the sun's rays fell at an angle of about 7°. He correctly assumed that the Sun is very far from Earth, making the rays that hit Earth almost parallel to one another. By measuring the length of the shadow cast on an object in Alexandria and knowing the distance between Alexandria and Syene he used geometry to determine Earth's diameter and circumference.

A versatile scholar, Eratosthenes also measured the tilt of Earth's axis (which gives us the four seasons), created a crude **map** of the world, and discovered a way to find all the prime numbers (a prime number has only two factors, itself and 1) in a list from 1 to any desired whole number.

Ericsson, John

Engineer: designed the *Monitor*
Born: July 31, 1803, Langban Shyttan, Sweden
Died: March 8, 1889, New York, New York

Ericsson began as a self-taught engineer in the Swedish army, but in 1826 decided to bring his inventions to England, the heart of the Industrial Revolution. His steam locomotive *Novelty* competed in a famous 1829 competition won by George Stephenson's *Rocket*. The *Novelty* was faster but unreliable; *Rocket* won on the basis of strength and dependability. Fame from the contest, however, made it easier for Ericsson to obtain backing for other inventions. These soon included a steam-powered fire engine and in 1839 his first iron ship, whose steam engine turned the screw propeller he had developed two years earlier.

In 1849, Ericsson built the *Princeton* for

The Monitor and the Merrimac battled off Norfolk, Virginia in 1862.

the U.S. Navy, the first iron-hulled, propeller-driven warship. The *Princeton* was also the first to have its engines below decks, making them safer from enemy fire. Unfortunately, a gun explosion during the official government inspection discouraged the navy from using the *Princeton* in action, even though the gun that exploded was not designed or built by Ericsson.

In 1862, during the U.S. Civil War, the Confederacy launched its own ironclad ship, the *Merrimack*, which promptly sank two Union vessels. Then it faced the *Monitor*, Ericsson's newly built iron ship. The *Monitor* was notable for the first rotating gun turret, which enabled it to defeat (but not sink) the *Merrimack*. After the war, all the world's navies built imitations of the *Monitor*.

Ericsson continued to pour forth inventions, including devices to use tidal and solar power and to extract salt from seawater.

 **RESOURCES**

• MORE ABOUT JOHN ERICSSON.

http://www.yahooligans.com/ Science_and_Nature/Machines/Inventions/ Inventors/Ericsson__John/

Evolution

Lucretius (idea that organisms can change) ➤ Erasmus Darwin, **LAMARCK** (acquired characteristics can be inherited) ➤ **CHARLES DARWIN/WALLACE** (observations led to today's understanding of evolution)

 The concept that new species of organisms develop as existing species gradually change is called evolution. The idea that organisms can change was proposed by some early philosophers, most notably Lucretius [Roman: c. 95–55 B.C.E.], who said that some animals have special adaptations that help them survive while

Chimpanzees and humans are believed to have evolved from a common ancestor some 5 million to 7 million years ago.

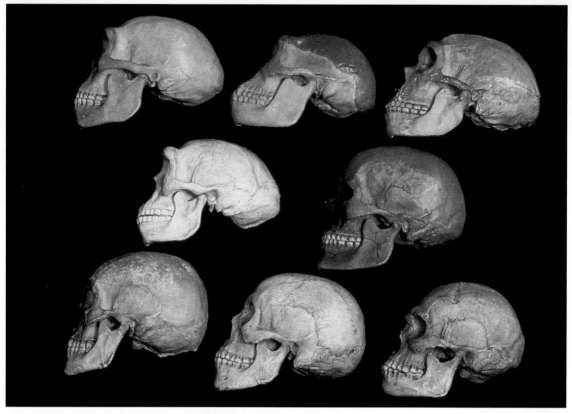

The theory of evolution can be applied to the characteristics of these skulls.

other animals are less fitted to survive and so become extinct. Most people, however, believed that each species of organism came into being as a result of a special and separate creation, and did not change through the ages.

But by the 18th century, scientists had gathered much evidence that organisms do indeed change over time. As the Americas were explored, many animal and plant species appeared that were different from, yet remarkably similar to, species in Europe, Asia, and Africa. Studies of rock layers showed that the oldest rocks contain **fossils** of simple organisms only, while younger rocks contain increasingly more complex species.

In the late 1700s Erasmus Darwin [English: 1731–1802; grandfather of Charles Darwin] wrote that species change because characteristics acquired during an organism's life—bigger muscles,

Notable Quotable

We are the product of 4.5 billion years of fortuitous, slow biological evolution. There is no reason to think that the evolutionary process has stopped. Man is a transitional animal. He is not the climax of creation.

—Carl Sagan

Nothing in biology makes sense except in the light of evolution.

—Theodosius Dobzhansky

for example—can be inherited by the organism's offspring. This mechanism for evolution was more fully developed by **Jean-Baptiste Lamarck** in 1809 and had many followers. However, genetic research has since proven that acquired characteristics cannot be inherited.

The mechanism of evolution accepted today is based on the observations of **Charles Darwin** and **Alfred Russel Wallace**, and documented by Darwin in *On the Origin of Species*, published in 1859. This theory of natural selection says there is much variety among individuals of a species. Individuals with variations that help in the struggle for survival are more likely to reproduce and pass on their variations than less well-endowed individuals. In time, some traits in the species become accentuated and other traits disappear.

Today, the theory of natural selection is a central principle of biology, strongly supported by a vast array of evidence. The ever-growing fossil record documents the evolutionary development of humans, horses, and many other kinds of organisms. Similarities in body chemistry and structures among diverse species, such as the bones in a human arm and a robin's wing, suggest common ancestors. The strongest and most direct evidence comes from genetics—a field that did not exist in Darwin's time. Beginning in the 20th century, scientists showed how **mutations** in **genes** can lead to new variations and how different species share common sequences of **DNA**. In laboratories they have tracked evolution at the molecular level in organisms that reproduce and mutate rapidly, particularly certain bacteria and viruses.

 RESOURCES

* Fortey, Richard. *Life: A Natural History of the First Four Billion Years of Life on Earth*. New York: Alfred P. Knopf, 1998.
* Gould, Stephen Jay. *The Book of Life: An Illustrated History of the Evolution of Life on Earth*. 2nd ed. New York: W.W. Norton, 2001.
* Howells, W.W. *Getting Here: The Story of Human Evolution*. Washington, DC: Compass, 1997.
* CHRONOLOGY OF EVOLUTION.
* **http://www.accessexcellence.org/AE/AEPC/ WWC/1995/cron_evol.html**

Explosives

China (first artificial explosive) ➤ **Europe** (second artificial explosive) ➤ **Schönbein** (guncotton) ➤ **Sobreo** (nitroglycerine) ➤ **NOBEL** (dynamite)

 Explosives explode; that is, they bang loudly and destroy nearby objects with a rush of expanding, very hot gas formed by rapid burning. By 850 C.E., Chinese experimenters had developed an early form of the first artificial explosive, gunpowder. Over the next 300 years, they gradually learned to make bombs, rockets, and guns that use gunpowder. Word of this reached Europe by at least 1268 because

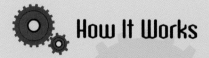 **How It Works**

Gunpowder mixes small amounts of powdered sulfur and charcoal into saltpeter (potassium nitrate). Sulfur ignites easily, heating the saltpeter and charcoal. Saltpeter releases oxygen, causing all three ingredients to burn faster. Gunpowder turns into very hot gas, expanding in volume by 3,000 times in the process.

Explosive bombs used as fireworks

Roger Bacon wrote of gunpowder in that year. The key ingredient in gunpowder, a mineral called saltpeter, is uncommon in Europe, however, so use of gunpowder was rare at first.

A second artificial explosive, called fulminate of gold, was discovered in Europe sometime before 1628. Several other metal fulminates (silver and mercury) share with gold fulminate the power to explode as a result of a sharp blow.

Dynamite set to explode when electricity sparks

In 1846, Christian Schönbein [German-Swiss: 1799–1868] accidentally discovered another unstable explosive, guncotton, when he spilled acids on cloth, and Ascanio Sobreo [Italian: 1812–1888] found nitro-glycerine by dripping the same acids into glycerin. Both guncotton and nitroglycerine are more powerful than gunpowder but less stable, as they explode easily from the slightest spark or shock. **Alfred Nobel** made nitroglycerine useful by converting it to more stable dynamite, while guncotton was modified to form "smokeless gunpowder."

Chemists in the 20th century created many more powerful explosives, such as trinitrotoluene (TNT) and plastic explosives, nearly all based on nitrogen-oxygen compounds.

See also fireworks.

 RESOURCES

- Akhavan, J. *The Chemistry of Explosives.* New York: Springer-Verlag, 1998.
- Brown, G.I. and Adam Hart Davis. *The Big Bang: A History of Explosives.* New York: Sutton, 2000.
- MORE ABOUT EXPLOSIVES.
  http://www.ordnance.org/explosives.htm
  http://www.ime.org/commercialindstry.htm

Extrasolar Planets

Knowledge that the Sun is a star gradually emerged during the 1700s and 1800s. Since the Sun is orbited by planets, people began to think that other stars might also have planets. A planet near another star, however, is lost in the star's brightness and is invisible from Earth. But by the 1990s, astronomers developed telescopes sensitive enough to detect extrasolar planets—planets around a star other than our Sun—from the effects of gravity. A planet in orbit about a star first pulls the star one way and then the other, producing a small wobble in the star. Using the wobble method, astronomers have found more than 60 such planets.

Known extrasolar planets are all very large. The smallest are almost as large as Saturn, the second-largest planet in this solar system. Most orbit very close to the star. A small orbit and large size combine to produce a faster and larger wobble, making the planet easier to detect. As better telescopes are built, it will become possible to find planets that are smaller and farther from their stars and therefore more like Earth.

 RESOURCES

- Clark, Stuart. *Extrasolar Planets: The Search for New Worlds.* New York: John Wiley, 1998.
- Crosswell, Ken. *Planet Quest: The Epic Discovery of Alien Solar Systems.* New York: Oxford University, 1998 (paperback, San Diego: Harcourt Brace, 1998).
- Lewis, John S. *Worlds without End: The Exploration of Planets Known and Unknown.* Cambridge, MA: Perseus, 1999.
- MORE ABOUT EXTRASOLAR PLANETS.
  http://cfa-www.harvard.edu/planets/
  http://astron.berkeley.edu/gmarcy/science_news_aug98.html
  http://www.public.asu.edu/sciref/exoplnt.htm

Fabre, Jean Henri

Entomologist: set new standards for observing nature
Born: December 22, 1823, St-Léons, France
Died: October 11, 1915, Sérignan, France

 Fabre was a university student when he became interested in entomology (the study of insects). At that time, entomologists typically studied collections of carefully preserved dead insects. Fabre wanted to study living insects in their natural environments.

Fabre taught for a while but retired while still relatively young. He moved to a small house that had a garden in which he could watch insects. His patience and highly accurate records set new standards for biologists. Fabre also was a good writer and one of the first popular science writers. His most famous work was *Souvenirs Entomologiques* [Entomological Recollections]. This 10-volume work, published between 1879 and 1907, described the anatomy, life cycles, and behavior of wasps, bees, grasshoppers, and many other insects.

 RESOURCES

- Fabre, Jean-Henri. *Bramble Bees and Others.* Poughkeepsie, NY: Vivisphere, 2000.
- Fabre, Jean-Henri. *Fabre's Book of Insects.* Mineola, NY: Dover, 1998.
- Fabre, Jean-Henri. *The Life of the Caterpillar.* Poughkeepsie, NY: Vivisphere, 2000.
- Fabre, Jean-Henri. *The Passionate Observer: Writings from the World of Nature.* San Francisco: Chronicle, 1998.

Fabricus, Hieryonimus

Anatomist: helped found embryology
Born: c. 1533, Aquapendente, Italy
Died: May 21, 1619, Bugazzi, Italy

Fabricius was among the first scientists to study embryos and their development. He was the first to describe the placenta (the organ in female mammals that connects the embryo to the uterus). He followed the development of a chick embryo from shortly after fertilization to hatching, and compared the anatomy of the embryos of cats, dogs, horses, and humans.

Fabricius wrote many papers on human **anatomy**, describing the larynx, lens of the eye, and other structures. Of greatest significance was his 1603 account of the

Human fetus

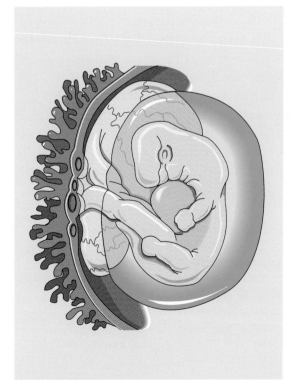

Hieryonimus Fabricus

semilunar valves in blood veins. However, he incorrectly believed that the purpose of these valves was to prevent blood from collecting in the arms and legs. One of his students, **William Harvey,** later determined the valves' true function: to prevent backflow of blood.

FAMOUS FIRST

In medical school Fabricius was the favorite pupil of Gabriele Falloppio [Italian: 1523–1562], who was the first person to describe many structures of human anatomy, including the tubes that connect a female human's ovaries to her uterus—now known as Fallopian tubes.

RESOURCES

- An Anatomy Lesson.
  http://gwis2.circ.gwu.edu/atkins/
  newwebpages/anatomylessons.html

Faraday, Michael

Physicist and chemist: discovered electromagnetic
induction
Born: September 22, 1791, Newington, England
Died: August 25, 1867, London, England

  Early in his career Faraday
worked with **Humphry Davy**
and became interested in the
relationships between electricity and
magnetism. In 1831, Faraday found that
he could induce an electric current in a
coil of copper wire by moving a magnet
in and out of the coil. The stronger the
magnet and the faster the magnet moved,
the greater the current produced. This
electromagnetic induction is the principle
behind electric generators and transformers. Its discovery by Faraday helped
change electricity from a curiosity into a
practical, powerful technology.

Faraday described a magnetic field
as being composed of invisible lines of
force. It is the "cutting" of these lines
by the coil of wire that creates the
current. Faraday also believed that
electricity is a form of force—not a fluid,
as was then widely believed. He proposed
the field theory of electromagnetism,
which was later fully developed by **James
Clerk Maxwell.**

Faraday's many contributions to
science also include liquefying chlorine
(1823), discovering benzene (1825),
stating the basic laws of **electrolysis**
(1832), and observing that the **polarization**

Michael Faraday

(plane of vibrations) of light changes
when exposed to a magnetic field (1845).
He coined many terms now widely used,
including ion, anode, cathode, electrode,
and electrolyte.

RESOURCES

- Fullick, Ann. *Michael Faraday.* Westport, CT:
  Heinemann, 2000. (JUV/YA)
- Russell, Colin Archibald. *Michael Faraday.* New
  York: Oxford University, 2000. (JUV/YA)
- Michael Faraday's "On Electrical Decomposition."
  http://dbhs.wvusd.k12.ca.us/Chem-History/
  Faraday-electrochem.html
- Michael Faraday (1791–1867).
  http://www.ri.ac.uk/History/M.Faraday/
  Home.html

Farming

 Domestication of plants and animals ➤ **Mesopotamia and China** (plows) ➤ **China** (manure/1st pesticide)   Metal tools ➤ **Tull** (mechanical seed drill/improved plows) ➤ Animal-drawn devices ➤ **MCCORMICK** (reaper) ➤ **de Laval** (commercial milking machine)

The **Agricultural Revolution** of about 9000 B.C.E. led to farming as a way of life. After **domestication** of plants and animals, most societies ceased to depend on hunting and gathering.

Early farming required few tools. Grain farmers used curved stone knives called sickles to harvest seeds and pairs of stones to grind seeds into flour. Soil was broken and weeds cut down with hoes. Some seeds or tubers were planted with sharpened sticks, while others were scattered on broken ground. By 4000 B.C.E., farmers in both Mesopotamia and China began to use plows in addition to hoes. A plow breaks up soil faster and deeper than a hoe can. Early plows were curved pieces of wood that humans or cattle pulled while a person behind pushed the blade down and guided it. By 2000 B.C.E. some farmers were drilling holes in plows for seeds; seeds could be funneled into the holes as the farmer plowed the field. Devices like this are called seed drills.

Farmers grew crops and tended animals, using part of the harvest to feed animals, which in turn supplied meat and milk. In China by 500 B.C.E. another use for farm animals was found; animal waste, called manure, was applied to fields as fertilizer, making crops grow faster and larger. By 100 B.C.E. Chinese farmers employed the

A modern harvester

Cattle provide milk, meat, and manure.

first pesticide, dried chrysanthemum leaves.

Metal tools eventually replaced stone and wood, at least for wealthier farmers, but there was little other change until just before the **Industrial Revolution**. Jethro Tull [English: 1674–1741] developed a mechanical seed drill in 1701 and later improved plows, combining several types into a single device. By the 1800s, inventive farmers and blacksmiths began to develop new animal-drawn devices for mowing hay or turning over weeds (called cultivating). Among the most famous was a harvesting machine called a reaper invented in 1831 by **Cyrus McCormick.**

Engine-based farming got a late start. Steam engines are too heavy for most farm operations. The first successful tractor, an all-purpose self-propelled farm vehicle, was introduced in 1901. Tractors not only replaced animals in pulling farm machinery, but also used attachments to power other equipment. In 1938, the self-propelled combine—a machine that harvests a crop and in the same operation separates useful grain or beans from the rest of the plant—was introduced.

Although most farm equipment concerned crops, there were a few innovations that affected animal farming. One was barbed wire, invented in 1867, which provided the first inexpensive fencing. In 1913, Gustaf de Laval [Swedish: 1845–1913] introduced a commercial milking machine.

The modern large farm operates like a factory for producing food. Fields are leveled using lasers, and sensors measure soil moisture, automatically turning irrigation machines on and off. Machine-fed animals mature in small stalls designed to let manure flow out automatically. These practices have resulted in ever-greater yields of food per farmer. As a result, farmers, once the bulk of the population, have been greatly reduced in number. Furthermore, environmentalists often criticize factory farms for the way they handle pesticides, irrigation, wastes, and genetically altered crops.

See also genetic engineering.

 **RESOURCES**

• Halberstadt, Hans. *The American Family Farm.* Osceola, WI: Motorbooks International, 1996.
• Hurt, R. Douglas. *American Agriculture: A Brief History.* Ames, IA: Iowa State University, 1994.
• Leffingwell, Randy. *Farm Tractor Milestones.* Osceola, WI: Motorbooks International, 2000.
• MORE ABOUT FARMING.
  http://www.worldfarming.com/

Philo T. Farnsworth

Farnsworth, Philo T.

Inventor: transmitted first television image
Born: August 19, 1906, Indian Creek, Utah
Died: March 11, 1971, Holladay, Utah

 Farnsworth grew up on a farm, where his chores included plowing hay and potato fields. One day in 1921, thinking about his favorite topic, science, as he plowed a row, turned the plow, started the next row, and repeated this pattern, he had a flash of insight. Why couldn't a camera be made that could create images consisting of row after row of electrons? Why couldn't these images then be transmitted and received row after row?

In 1922, Farnsworth described his idea to his science teacher, accompanying his ex-planations with drawings. The teacher was so impressed that he kept one of Farnsworth's sketches. This sketch was a deciding factor in a 1934 patent dispute, for it proved that Farnsworth was the first person to define the basic requirements of **television**.

After two years of college, Farnsworth began research on picture transmission and in 1926 set up a laboratory in San

YEARBOOK: 1927

- Farnsworth applies for patents for his camera and receiving system.
- Rolex introduces the first waterproof watch.
- The first commercial **motion picture** with spoken dialogue—The Jazz Singer— is released.

Francisco. There, on September 7, 1927, he transmitted the first television image—a picture of his wife and assistant, Pem. Later in 1927, he transmitted the first motion image—a puff of smoke from a cigarette.

Farnsworth invented numerous additional devices, including cathode-ray tubes, a simple electron microscope, a sterile crib for premature babies, and a system for air traffic control.

 RESOURCES

- McPherson, Stephanie Sammartino. *TV's Forgotten Hero: The Story of Philo Farnsworth.* Minneapolis: Carolrhoda, 1996. (JUV/YA)

- MORE ABOUT PHILO T. FARNSWORTH.

  http://farnovision.com/chronicles/

  http://www.inventorsmuseum.com/television.htm

  http://philotfarnsworth.com/

Fasteners for Clothing

Plant fibers, sinews, skins ➤ leather belts ➤ bone pins ➤ **Sumerians** (iron pins) ➤ **Romans** (early safety pin; early button) ➤ **Hunt** (re-invented safety pin) ➤ **DE MESTRAL** (Velcro)

 Plant fibers, animal sinews (tendons), and straps cut from skins appear to have been the first universal fasteners that could be easily closed and opened. Tied-together skins may have formed the first clothing. Because fibers and leather decay easily, evidence is rare. Recognizable awls for punching holes in leather date from 20,000 B.C.E. Rope marks are found in the cave at Lascaux, left about 15,000 B.C.E. Danes, from evidence 4,000 years old preserved in bogs, kept loincloths in place with leather belts—but the earliest known Danish buckle dates from about 1400 B.C.E. The Ice Man, a body preserved in an

Italian glacier since 3300 B.C.E., used sinews and grass to fasten clothing together and to lace shoes.

Early people also used pins as fasteners. Bone and iron pins were used to hold clothing together by Sumerians in Mesopotamia from 3000 B.C.E. Romans about 500 B.C.E. even developed a form of safety pin, although the idea was lost until re-invented in 1849 by Walter Hunt [American: 1796–1859]. The Romans also employed buttons, which fit into loops. Buttonholes did not come into use in Europe until the Middle Ages (about 1250 C.E.).

Even today, most clothing is held together with strings, belts, and buttons, although modern times have added the **zipper** and **George De Mestral's** Velcro.

Buttons have been used since Roman times.

Fax Machines

Bain (paper to receive) ➤ **Caselli** (first tranmissions) ➤ **Korn** (photoelectric system) ➤ **Belin** (first machine to use telephone lines) ➤ **Xerox Corporation** (first easy office fax) ➤ **Canon Corporation** (fax/copiers)

A facsimile—or fax—machine

 Transmission of images by telegraph preceded modern facsimile, or fax, machines. Early versions used a combination of conducting and insulating materials to create the original image, to which electric current was applied. The current was then transmitted as an on-or-off pattern to the machine at the receiving end, which repeated the pattern of motion of the sending mechanism point by point. Alexander Bain [Scottish: 1810–1877] in 1840 devised chemically treated paper for the receiving end; it changes color in response to electric current. By 1861, Giovanni Caselli [Italian: 1815–1891] created a working system that transmitted images produced with insulating ink. France employed Caselli's system, starting in 1865, with lines connecting Paris to Lyon and Marseilles. These shut down in 1870 because of a war.

In 1902, Arthur Korn [German: 1870–1945] invented a system based on photoelectric phenomena that eliminated special preparation of images since it responded to changes in light reflected from black ink or white paper. A commercial version was instituted in Germany in 1907, from Munich to Berlin.

Also in 1907, Edouard Belin [French: 1876–1963] developed the first machine to use telephone lines for images. His portable Belinograph, or "Belino," of 1913 became a standard tool of newspapers from the 1920s through the 1950s. Other inventors converted the telephone-based Belino to facsimile machines that transmitted images by radio.

In 1966, the Xerox Corporation introduced the first easy-to-use office fax, which used telephone transmission like the Belino and a special paper that responds to heat to reproduce images. International standards for telephone-based faxes, starting in 1974, allowed machines from different manufacturers to interact. In 1987, Canon introduced fax machines that make copies on ordinary paper, using **document copying** technology based on xerography. And in 1985, personal computers provided a new way to send and receive faxes, working with desktop printers capable of reproducing any images.

 RESOURCES

- HISTORIES OF FACSIMILE MACHINES.

  http://www.hffax.de/History/hauptteil_faxhistory.html

  http://library.thinkquest.org/27887/gather/history/fax.shtml

  http://www.ideafinder.com/history/inventions/story051.htm

- BIOGRAPHY OF GIOVANNI CASELLI.

  http://www.cinemedia.net/SFCV-RMIT-Annex/rnaughton/CASELLI_BIO.html

Fermentation

For at least 10,000 years people have known that certain foods change when left in a warm, dark place for a period of time. In this manner ancient people made bread, wine, beer, yogurt, and other edibles. Because such foods often give off bubbles of gas, they are said to ferment (derived from the Latin for "to boil").

It wasn't until 1697 that Georg Ernst Stahl [German: 1660–1734] suggested that fermentation is a chemical process. In 1793,

Antoine-Laurent Lavoisier agreed, noting that the fermentation that produces wine involves a breakdown of sugar in grapes.

Yeast cells were first seen in 1680 by Antoni van Leeuwenhoek when he looked at beer through his microscope. He didn't realize, however, that yeast are living organisms and can cause fermentation. **Theodor Schwann** demonstrated this in 1836 but the reports of **Louis Pasteur**, beginning in 1856, were what convinced people that yeast and certain other microorganisms growing in the absence of oxygen are the cause of fermentation.

In the late 1890s Eduard Buchner [German: 1860–1917] ground up yeast cells, producing a cell-free juice. He demonstrated that this juice contains

Grapes are fermented to make wine.

the substances that cause fermentation. Today we know that these substances are **enzymes**.

RESOURCES

• Louis Pasteur, "Physiological Theory of Fermentation."
http://www.fordham.edu/halsall/mod/1879pasteur-ferment.html

Fermi, Enrico

Physicist: designed and built first nuclear reactor
Born: September 29, 1901, Rome, Italy
Died: November 28, 1954, Chicago, Illinois

 Fermi was the only physicist of the 20th century whose experimental and theoretical work are equally valuable.

In the 1920s, Fermi used mathematics to analyze the ways in which **subatomic particles** of matter, such as electrons and protons, interact in large collections. Such particles are now called fermions and their rules of interaction, Fermi-Dirac statistics (Paul Dirac [British: 1902–1984] was a Nobel Prize-winning physicist who theorized about quantum mechanics). Among Fermi's other contributions to atomic theory was the only name for a particle derived from Italian, the neutrino ("little neutral one"). Fermi also explained the origin of many properties of metals on the basis of electrons.

NOBEL PRIZE 1938

Fermi received the Nobel Prize in physics for the discovery of effects of slow-moving neutrons on elements and isotopes.

Enrico Fermi

Fermi turned from theory to experimental work in 1932 and showed that slow-moving neutrons can change one element into another. In the 1930s, the Italian government allied itself with Germany, which was treating Jews harshly. Fermi's wife was Jewish, so the Fermis emigrated to the

FAMOUS FIRST

Fermi built the first nuclear reactor as part of a secret weapons program. His reactor demonstrated that once atoms begin splitting, their energy can split other atoms in a controlled "chain reaction." The U.S. president was told with the following coded message about this finding: "the Italian navigator has reached shore safely and found the natives friendly."

United States. In 1942, Fermi was the chief designer of the first working **nuclear reactor,** based on techniques that he developed to control nuclear fission in uranium. Fermi's reactor was essential to the building of the first **nuclear weapons**.

 RESOURCES

• Cooper, Dan. *Enrico Fermi and the Revolutions of Modern Physics* (Oxford Portraits in Science). New York: Oxford Children's, 1998.

• ENRICO FERMI.

  http://www.almaz.com/nobel/physics/1938a.html

Fertilizers

💡 **Humboldt** (introduced guano) ➤ **1800s/1900s** (scientists identify chemicals essential to plant growth) ➤ **DAVY** (compendium of plant-growing knowledge) ➤ **Lawes** (artificial fertilizer) ➤ **Gilbert** (determined nutritional needs of crops)

 Fertilizers are substances added to soil to help plants grow. They contain nitrogen, phosphorus, and other elements needed for plentiful, healthy growth.

Thousands of years ago, long before plant nutrition was understood, people noticed that soils used over and over again for agriculture produced ever-poorer crops. They also saw that when substances such as wood ashes and animal manure were added to the soil, plant growth improved. In 1804, Alexander von Humboldt [German: 1769–1859] introduced guano, a dried bird manure abundant on islands off Peru, to Europe, where it became a principal fertilizer for most of the 1800s.

It wasn't until the 1800s and early 1900s that scientists identified all the chemical elements essential for plant growth. Much of this work was motivated by **Humphry Davy's** 1813 publication of *Elements of Agricultural Chemistry*, a compendium of knowledge to date.

In 1842, John Bennet Lawes [English: 1814–1900] patented a process for treating phosphate rock to produce superphosphate,

A modern tractor and harvester

thereby founding the artificial fertilizer industry. In 1843, he established a factory near London to produce superphosphate. Together with J. H. Gilbert [English: 1817–1901] he spent the rest of the 1800s conducting field tests and chemical analyses to determine the specific nutritional needs of various crop plants.

Today, precise tests indicate the supply of nutrients in soils and what should be added. Both natural and artificial fertilizers are used, greatly improving crop production.

RESOURCES
• FERTILIZERS
  http://tomgreen-ext.tamu.edu/mg/fertiliz.htm

Fiber Optics

 Kapany (idea that glass can transmit light) ➤ Development of lasers ➤ Development of endoscopes ➤ Development of fiber-optic cable

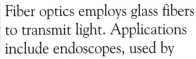 Fiber optics employs glass fibers to transmit light. Applications include endoscopes, used by physicians to peer inside body organs;

periscopes for military vehicles from **submarines** to tanks; and cables that carry most long-distance telephone messages. The recognition that glass fibers can transmit light for long distances and around curves occurred to Narinder S. Kapany [Indian: 1927–] in 1951, although the basic principle had long been known. Development of **lasers** during the 1950s greatly increased the power of optical equipment.

Endoscopes revolutionized surgery, permitting operations through small openings. Fibers carry light to the interior of the body or images to the surgeon, sometimes with the aid of tiny television cameras. Many specialized endoscopes, such as colonoscopes for examination of the colon, part of the large intestine, include tools for removal of growths observed during diagnosis. The future of fiber optics may include use in optical computers.

Fiber-optic cables carry many messages at once because electromagnetic waves combine as one signal but easily separate at the receiving end. Messages transmitted by light are subject to less distortion than

Thin optical fibers carry as many messages as several large metal cables.

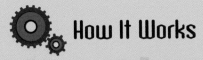

How It Works

A fiber-optic cable transmits light around curves and with little loss of strength because of total internal reflection of light. When light strikes the boundary between substances, it bends. If light's angle to the boundary is low enough, it bends back instead of passing through the boundary. An example of this is when an image of trees is reflected in the still water of a pond. The outer casing of fiber optic cables is a material chosen to optimize the angle at which light bounces back into the glass fiber.

those carried by electric currents, which encounter static from stray electromagnetic fields and can be affected by temperature.

 RESOURCES

- Crisp, John. *Introduction to Fiber Optics.* Newton, MA: Butterworth-Heinemann, 1997.
- Hecht, Jeff. *City of Light: The Story of Fiber Optics.* New York: Oxford University, 1999.
- INTRODUCTION TO FIBER OPTICS FOR COMMUNICATIONS.

  http://www.commspecial.com/
  fiberguide.htm

  http://oak.cats.ohiou.edu/sl302186/fiber.html

Fibers

Early humans (animal fibers) ➤ Wild flax plant ➤ Domesticated sheep and goats for wool ➤ **India / Peru** (cotton fiber) ➤ **China** (silk) ➤ **Asia** (hemp) ➤ Early spinning with hand tools ➤ **China** (spinning wheel) ➤ **HOOKE** (idea to imitate natural silkmaking) ➤ Development of cellulose ➤ **Chardonnet** (rayon) ➤ **CAROTHERS** (nylon) ➤ Development of polyester ➤ Development of permanent press

 Fibers are threadlike strands, such as those that make cloth or rope. Short fibers are the basis of **paper** and stiff or strong fibers are

used in **composites**. After food, fibers—natural and artificial—have been a main goal of hunters, farmers, and, more recently, chemists.

Early humans, at least by 15,000 B.C.E. and probably much earlier, used animal fibers in two ways—sinews formed the earliest string or rope, while animal fur, still attached to the skin, warmed bodies as clothing and as part of shelter. In central Europe around 10,000 B.C.E., people harvested the wild flax plant—the source of linen fiber and linseed oil. Grasses were sometimes used as fibers in that region, based on clothing on a body from 3300 B.C.E. preserved in an Italian glacier. At the eastern end of the Mediterranean Sea, goats and sheep were among the first animals to be domesticated, around 9000 B.C.E. The fibers that cover these animals form wool. Cotton fiber comes from plants that were domesticated in both India and Peru about 3000 B.C.E. Silk, an animal fiber

A loom for weaving fiber into cotton.

Sheep provide wool.

produced by caterpillars and spiders, became available in China when the silkworm, the caterpillar of a moth, was domesticated about 3000 B.C.E. Hemp, used more for rope than cloth, is another important early fiber of Asia.

Below left: *Flax in flower;* **Below right:** *A cotton ball*

Natural fibers are too short for nearly all purposes, so they must be twisted into long threads by spinning. The fibers are first cleaned and separated from other materials, such as seeds or stems, and then combed parallel. Most early spinning was done with no tools at all or with simple hand tools. The spinning wheel is a comparatively late invention—known in China by 1030 C.E. and in the West by 1280, but based on an earlier type of wheel from India. Spun fiber, whose technical name is yarn, is made into cloth by **weaving**. The word textile (from the Latin for "weave") refers to both yarn and cloth.

In 1665, **Robert Hooke** observed that it should be possible to imitate the method animals use to make silk by extruding a suitable liquid through small holes and letting it solidify. Nearly 200 years later, cellulose, a substance extracted from wood, became the first source of a suitable liquid for Hooke's idea. The first experimenters could not make commercially acceptable textiles from cellulose, but in 1884, Comte Hilaire Bernigaud de Chardonnet [French: 1839–1924] succeeded, producing an artificial silk called rayon. By 1892, several improved versions of rayon were being manufactured.

In 1935, **Wallace Hume Carothers** invented nylon, a plastic that can be made into a textile that is better than silk for many purposes. A different plastic-based fiber, polyester, was developed in England in 1940. Dacron, the first polyester, is more heat-resistant than nylon, more durable than rayon, and takes **dyes** better than either. In 1964, a polyester textile that never needs ironing, called

permanent press, was introduced. Today, many fabrics combine natural and artificial textiles to take advantage of the best qualities of each.

 **RESOURCES**

- MORE ABOUT NATURAL FIBERS.
  http://daphne.palomar.edu/wayne/traug99.htm
  http://www.utexas.edu/depts/bbr/natfiber/

Fire

 Control of fire sets humans apart from other animals. Fire provides warmth and **lighting**; makes food more digestible while killing infectious agents; hardens wood for better weapons; clears forests for farming; smelts metals; and creates bricks and pots from clay.

The first use of fire dates from more than one million years ago.

Advances in civilization seem to require technology based on the use of fire.

Human control of fire appears very early, long before *Homo sapiens*. The earliest evidence of hearths—fire-hardened clay and layers of ash—dates from more than a million years ago. At first, fires were probably kept alight by continually providing fuel, but early people learned that rapid rotation of a stick against another piece of wood produces enough heat to start fire anew. Sparks produced by striking flint against iron pyrites also light easily flammable materials. This method is still used in some devices to ignite flammable fluids. **Matches**, which use chemicals to ignite fire, were introduced in the early 1800s and remain common today.

Control of fire includes prevention of fire. Large fires, such as building or forest fires, are still extinguished with water, but chemical fire extinguishers, such as those that produce carbon dioxide, invented starting in 1866, are used to halt smaller unwanted fires.

 **RESOURCES**

- Pyne, Stephen J. *World Fire: The Culture of Fire on Earth*. Seattle: University of Washington, 1997.

Fireworks

 The Chinese originated fireworks, the production of loud bangs, brilliant colors, and soaring lights. The first Chinese fireworks used bamboo, which contains air in tight compartments and explodes with a loud bang when thrown into a fire. Bamboo fireworks graced Chinese celebrations as early

Golden trails from falling, burning fireworks stars

as 200 B.C.E. After the invention of the **explosive** called gunpowder about 850 C.E., the Chinese developed the original forms of all the fireworks used today—gunpowder-based devices that shoot colored streams or balls of fiery particles into the air (now

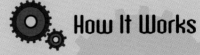 **How It Works**

The typical firework launches a casing called a shell skyward from a short cannon. The shell contains a small bomb and many stars—small bits that burn brilliantly in color for a few seconds. Lighting one fuse fires the cannon and ignites a second fuse in the shell. The second fuse explodes the bomb in the shell, igniting stars and propelling them outward.

known as fountains and Roman candles); devices propelled by streams of fire; and small bombs called firecrackers. The first gunpowder recipes did not explode with a bang, but burned rapidly, producing a whoosh. Adding different materials to the gunpowder created sparks of brilliant color. By about 1000 C.E., more powerful gunpowder made "thunderclap" bombs. The first rockets date from about 1150.

Fireworks spread to Europe, becoming especially popular in the 17th century. The Ruggeris of the 18th century and the Gruccis of the 20th are well-known Italian families specializing in large-scale fireworks shows. Although there have been no major technical advances in fireworks, each manufacturer has developed new ways to produce colors and special effects.

RESOURCES
- Plimpton, George. *Fireworks: A History and Celebration*. Garden City, NY: Doubleday, 1984.
- MORE ABOUT FIREWORKS.
  http://www.pbs.org/wgbh/nova/kaboom/

Fleming, Alexander

Bacteriologist: discovered penicillin
Born: August 6, 1881, Lochfield, Scotland
Died: March 11, 1955, London, England

 Fleming is best remembered for his discovery of penicillin. The son of a farmer, he studied to become a doctor and earned his medical degree, but decided that doing research would be more exciting. He made his first important discovery in 1921, finding an **enzyme** he called lysozyme in mucus from his nose. He later found lysozyme in other natural substances, including

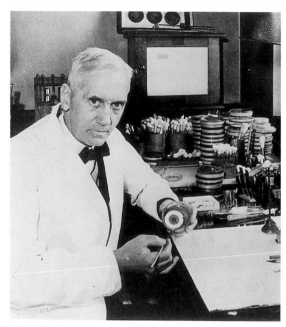
Alexander Fleming

human tears, chicken egg whites, and turnip juice.

In 1928, Fleming smeared some bacteria on lab dishes before taking a week's vacation. When he returned, he saw that one of the lab dishes had been contaminated with a mold, and that no bacteria were growing near the mold. He concluded that the mold produced a substance that killed bacteria.

NOBEL PRIZE 1945

Fleming, Florey, and Chain shared the Nobel Prize in physiology or medicine "for the discovery of penicillin and its curative effect in various infectious diseases."

He identified the mold as *Penicillium notatum* and named the substance penicillin. It was the first known **antibiotic**.

More than a decade passed before the importance of Fleming's discovery became apparent. In 1941, Howard Florey [British: 1898–1968] and Ernst Chain [British: 1906–1979] purified penicillin and produced sufficient quantities to test its effectiveness in fighting disease-causing bacteria. The tests were very successful and penicillin soon was used to save the lives of soldiers wounded in World War II. It remains one of the most widely used antibiotics.

 RESOURCES

- Gottfried, Ted. *Alexander Fleming: Discoverer of Penicillin*. Danbury, CT: Franklin Watts, 1997. (JUV/YA)
- BIOGRAPHY OF SIR ALEXANDER FLEMING.
  http://www.nobel.se/medicine/laureates/1945/fleming-bio.html

Fleming, John Ambrose

Electrical engineer: invented the diode
Born: November 29, 1849, Lancaster, England
Died: April 18, 1945, Sidmouth, England

  Fleming's best-known invention was the diode ("two-electrode") electronic tube, which he called the thermionic valve. It was based on a phenomenon described by **Thomas Alva Edison** in 1884, called the Edison effect: in a vacuum, electrons flow from a heated electrode (the cathode) to a cooler electrode (the anode). The diode, patented by Fleming in 1904, was the first implement to put the Edison effect to use. It changed the alternating current of **radio** signals into a direct current recognized by a receiver. The diode became a part of almost all radio transmitters and receivers, and was used in early **television** sets and **computers**. It also led to the development of other multi-electrode tubes, most impor-

John Ambrose Fleming

tantly the triode ("three electrode") invented by **Lee De Forest**.

Fleming's interest in science developed in childhood, and grew throughout his college years. Among Fleming's college teachers was **James Clerk Maxwell**, who awakened his interest in the practical applications of electricity. Fleming made improvements to electric meters, incandescent lamps, and electric generators. He also helped design the station in Cornwall, England, that transmitted the first transatlantic radio message.

 RESOURCES

- FLEMING'S ELECTRIC VALVE.
  http://www.uh.edu/engines/epi1323.htm
- JOHN AMBROSE FLEMING'S THERMIONIC "VALVE" (1904).
  http://www.deas.harvard.edu/jones/cscie129/lectures/lecture6/diodes/fleming.html

Fluorescence

Becquerel (fluorescent process) ➤ **Plücker** (electrically charged glass glows) ➤ **BOHR** (electrons changing orbit create light) ➤ **CROOKES** (neon lights)

Fluorescence is chemical production of light in response to energy, most familiar in fluorescent **lighting**, commercially introduced in 1938. Fluorescent tubes are more energy-efficient than incandescent bulbs because fluorescence produces light with almost no heat. The process used in fluorescent lamps was introduced in 1857 by Alexandre Becquerel [French: 1820–1891], but the specific chemicals needed for lighting homes and offices were difficult to develop.

Fluorescence also produces the images formed by cathode-ray tubes used as **displays** for television or computers, where beams of electrons cause chemicals on screens to glow. This was first observed by Julius Plücker [German: 1801–1868] in 1858 when he noticed that the glass struck by electrically charged particles glows. Further work led to the identification of cathode rays and the subsequent discovery of the

Fluorescent lights

electron in 1897, but it was not until 1913 that **Niels Bohr** showed that electrons changing orbit create light, the atomic basis of fluorescence.

 How It Works

Fluorescence occurs when relatively high energy is stored in the orbits of electrons around atoms and then released as electrons fall into lower orbits. For fluorescent lights a gas in the tube become ionized and releases ultraviolet radiation in response to an electric current. This radiation is invisible, but it induces chemicals coating the interior of the tube to re-release the energy as visible light.

Clouds of interstellar gas often fluoresce in response to the energy from starlight. Neon lights also are glowing gases, ionized by an electric current, an effect discovered in the 1870s by **William Crookes**.

See also electronics.

Food Preservation

Early humans (dried meat, fruit) ➤ **APPERT** (boiling and airtight) ➤ **PASTEUR** (microscopic organisms cause spoilage) ➤ **Carre** (refrigeration) ➤ **BIRDSEYE** (quick freezing) ➤ **France** (freeze-drying) ➤ Development of food irradiation ➤ Development of genetic altering

 Most food left at room temperature soon becomes unhealthy and unpleasant. Active compounds in food attack parts of cells when cells die. Bacteria and fungi grow on food, particularly when moisture is present, changing its chemical composition. The results include bitter or sour taste, loss of structure (food becomes soft and slimy), and in many cases disease.

Dried fruit is popular today.

Early humans dried meat or fruit in the sun or over a fire to produce food that does not decay for months. Smoke also preserves meat. Using a lot of salt or vinegar prevents food from rotting. Drying, smoking, salting, and pickling also change tastes and other properties of food.

In 1795, French Emperor Napoleon I offered a prize for a better way to preserve food. The contest was won by **Nicolas-Francis Appert**, who, in 1804, stopped decay by heating food above boiling and then sealing it in airtight containers. This method, called canning, is still popular. In the 1860s, **Louis Pasteur** showed that microscopic organisms cause food to spoil and that heating kills the microorganisms, which preserves food longer and prevents disease.

Cold also slows chemical action and growth of microorganisms. From ancient times, food was kept on ice or in cool places such as wells. The invention of refrigeration in 1857 by Ferdinand Carré [French: 1824–1900] made it easier to keep food cool. But cooling only delays decay for a few days. **Clarence Birdseye**, after observ-

Food can be preserved in airtight glass containers.

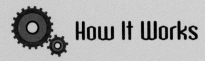

How It Works

For home canning (which typically uses glass jars, despite the name), acidic vegetables, such as tomatoes, are cooked to inactivate molecules that could attack cells, then put into heat-sterilized jars. Jars are loosely capped and heated to drive out air, which might harbor contaminants. Cooling then seals the jars airtight. Fruits are combined with sugar, which by itself prevents cells from collapsing and discourages bacteria and fungi. Other foods are pickled in vinegar and salt, both of which preserve them.

ing natural quick freezing in the far north, developed commercial frozen food starting in 1924. Once frozen, food stays usable for months. Frozen food was introduced in 1930 and became popular in the 1940s after home freezers became common.

In 1906, French scientists combined quick drying with freezing. Freeze-dried food can be kept at room temperature and when water is added becomes somewhat like fresh food. Freeze drying is expensive and the idea was abandoned until the U.S. Army began to freeze-dry orange juice in 1941. Freeze-dried products today are mostly carried by hikers.

In 1968, bacon and potatoes sterilized by exposure to radioactive cobalt-60 were manufactured, but radiation-preserved food did not reach the general public until the end of the 1990s. In 1997, the World Health Organization endorsed food irradiation. By early 2000, the U.S. Department of Agriculture had simplified its rules, allowing irradiated food to become common in the United States.

In 1994, the first food genetically altered to preserve itself, the Flavr Savr tomato, reached test markets, but it failed to catch on. It was declared a failure in 1997.

 RESOURCES

- Greene, Janet C. *Putting Food By*. New York: Penguin USA, 1992.
- McClure, Susan, ed. *Preserving Summer's Bounty: A Quick and Easy Guide to Freezing, Canning, Preserving, and Drying What You Grow*. Emmaus, PA: Rodale, 1998.
- Thorne, Stuart. *The History of Food Preservation*. New York: Barnes & Noble, 1986.
- THE NATIONAL FOOD SAFETY DATABASE.
  http://www.foodsafety.ufl.edu/index.html
- THE U.S. DEPARTMENT OF AGRICULTURE.
  http://www.nal.usda.gov/fnic/etext/000028.html

Food Pyramids and Chains

Thienemann (concepts of pyramids and chains) ➤ **Elton** (described energy passing between organisms) ➤ **CARSON** (effects of human activities on food chains)

 The concepts of food pyramids and chains were introduced to **ecology** during the 1920s. August Thienemann [German: 1882–1960] said communities have different feeding levels, with food energy transferred up from one level to the next. At the broad base of this pyramid are green plants and other food producers. Next come primary consumers, which eat the producers. Then come secondary consumers, which eat primary consumers. At the top are tertiary consumers, which eat secondary consumers. Later research demonstrated that at each higher level, the amount of available energy declines because most of the energy in

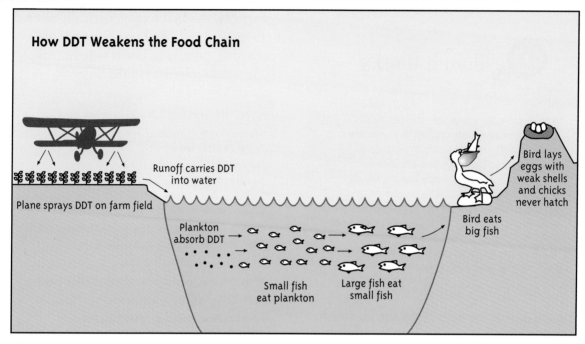

How DDT Weakens the Food Chain

Runoff carries DDT into water

Plane sprays DDT on farm field

Plankton absorb DDT →

Small fish eat plankton

Large fish eat small fish

Bird eats big fish

Bird lays eggs with weak shells and chicks never hatch

food is used for growth and metabolism or given off as heat and wastes. As a result, for every 1000 calories of food eaten by a primary consumer squirrel, only about 100 calories are available to the secondary consumer bobcat that eats the squirrel.

Charles Elton [English: 1900–1991] built on Thienemann's work, describing

Birds are at a higher level on the food chain than worms.

how energy passes from one organism to another in feeding links he called food chains. Because the organisms are linked together, what affects one species affects everything else in the chain. If a grassland is flooded, mice that eat grass seed either move elsewhere or die; hawks that eat mice also adjust or die. Every community has many overlapping food chains that form a food web. Hawks, for example, also eat rabbits and small birds.

In later decades, **Rachel Carson** and other scientists showed how human activities affect food chains. For instance, scientists reported in 2000 that mercury used to extract gold from ore during the California Gold Rush of the early 1850s is still part of food chains, found in the tissues of bass and other fish. Another area of recent interest has been the impact of non-native species—called alien or exotic species—on a community's food chains and webs.

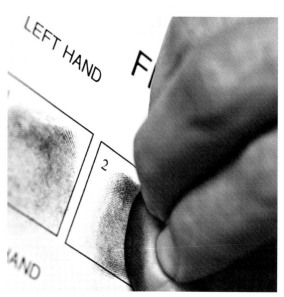
Fingerprinting was an early forensic technique.

early 20th centuries. In 1814, Mathieu Orfila [Spanish: 1787–1853] described how to detect and identify poisons. In the 1860s, chemical tests were developed to determine if a substance is blood. In 1900, England became the first country to use fingerprints to identify criminals. Albert S. Osborn [American: 1858–1946] developed the basic principles of examining letters, checks, and other documents, and in 1910

RESOURCES

- Bowler, Peter J. *The Earth Encompassed: A History of the Environmental Sciences.* New York: W.W. Norton, 2000.
- Elton, Charles S. *The Ecology of Invasions by Animals and Plants.* Chicago: University of Chicago, 2000.

Forensic Science

Orfila (how to detect and identify poisons) ➤ **England** (fingerprints) ➤ **Osborn** (letter and document examination) ➤ **Lattes** (blood group identification) ➤ Development of chromatography ➤ Development of computer fingerprint technology

Forensic science uses scientific methods to solve crimes. The field began in the 19th and

How It Works

Genetic profiling-sometimes called DNA fingerprinting-has been used since 1987 to help identify and convict murderers and other criminals. Except for identical twins, no two humans have the exact same DNA. By comparing the DNA in blood, sweat stains, and other evidence gathered at a crime scene with the DNA of a suspect, investigators can link the suspect to the crime or prove that the person is innocent.

Fossils

💡 **ARISTOTLE** (fossils as natural accidents) ➤ **DA VINCI/STENO** (recognized true nature of fossils) ➤ **HOOKE** (examined under microscope) ➤ **Guettard** (compared geology) ➤ **Smith** (examined rock layers, discovered distinctive fossils) ➤ **LAMARCK** (link to evolution) ➤ **Cuvier** (compared anatomy) ➤ **DARWIN** (theory of evolution) ➤ Development of radioactive dating ➤ Development of computer imaging

 Scientists have known about fossils since ancient times. It wasn't until the 18th century, however, that there was general agreement that fossils are remains of organisms that lived long ago. Some early Greeks believed fossils were mythological creatures. **Aristotle's** belief that fossils were natural accidents held sway for many centuries; for instance, Albertus Magnus [German: 1192–1280] called fossils "games of nature." A popular 17th-century theory claimed fossils were organisms trapped during the great flood described in the Bible.

published the first important book on this subject. In 1915, Leone Lattes [Italian: 1887–1954] developed a way to determine the blood group of a dried bloodstain.

Numerous advances in science and technology have produced powerful tools for gathering and analyzing crime information. Microscopes are used to study the color, shape, and scales of strands of hair. Chromatography identifies gasolines, paints, illicit drugs, and other chemicals. Computers convert fingerprints into digital data and store the information in databases; computerized analysis then locates stored prints that resemble a print found at a crime scene.

YEARBOOK: 1990

- In South Dakota, Sue Hendrickson [American-French: 1949–] uncovers the largest, most complete *Tyrannosaurus rex* dinosaur fossil ever found.
- The Hubble Space Telescope is launched.
- A four-year-old girl becomes the first person to receive human gene therapy.
- Tim Berners-Lee conceives the **World Wide Web**.

📺📖 RESOURCES

- Fridell, Ron. *Solving Crimes: The Pioneers of Forensic Science*. Danbury, CT: Franklin Watts, 2000. (JUV/YA)
- Owen, David, compiler. *Hidden Evidence: 41 True Crimes and How Forensic Science Helped Solve Them*. Pleasantville, NY: Reader's Digest, 1999.
- Thomas, Ronald R. *Detective Fiction and the Rise of Forensic Science*. New York: Cambridge University, 1999.

Leonardo da Vinci and **Nicolaus Steno** were among the few 15th-, 16th-, and 17th-century thinkers who recognized the true nature of fossils. **Robert Hooke**, the first person known to have examined fossils under a microscope, noticed similarities

Fossils—traces of ancient living things—show how Earth's climate and landscape have changed over time.

and differences between fossil and living mollusk shells and said that many fossils represent extinct organisms.

As more fossils were found, it became obvious that they couldn't all be "accidents" or results of a single flood. Jean Étienne Guettard [French: 1715–1786] compared the geology of northern France and southern England, noting that the two regions had very similar fossils and that the oldest fossils were in the deepest rocks while young fossils were near the surface.

In the 1790s, William Smith [English: 1769–1839] was supervising construction of a canal in northern England. He examined the rock layers exposed during excavation and saw that each layer had its own distinctive fossils. Some kinds of fossils occurred only in a single layer; others were in two or more adjacent layers. Smith also realized that the older the rock layer, the less its fossils resemble currently living creatures. Traveling around England, Smith repeatedly saw the same layers, with the same fossils. These discoveries that fossils formed in a definite sequence, not haphazardly, became the basis of the first system for dating rock layers and contributed to creation of the **geological time scale**.

In 1809, **Jean-Baptiste Lamarck** used fossils to advance the concept of **evolution**. "Is it not possible that these petrified individuals are the ancestors of species found

Notable Quotable

I always remember the first time I held in my hand the bone of a creature that had walked the earth millions of years before. I had dug it up myself. A feeling of awe crept over me. I thought, "Once this creature stood here. It was alive, had flesh and hair. It had its own smell. It could feel hunger and thirst and pain. It could enjoy the morning sun."

— Jane Goodall

today?" he wrote. Georges Cuvier [French: 1769-1832] rejected this possibility, but is called the founder of paleontology (the study of ancient life) because he was the first to systematically compare the **anatomy** of fossils and living organisms.

Publication of **Charles Darwin's** theory of evolution in 1859 profoundly influenced paleontologists. It fostered searches for so-called "missing links"—intermediate, transitional organisms between known species. The first such fossil was discovered in 1861. Named *Archaeopteryx*, it was a very primitive bird with characteristics of both its reptile ancestors and modern birds.

Various technologies introduced in the 20th century greatly expanded the study of fossils. The development of radioactive **dating** replaced Smith's comparative time scale with absolute measurements, enabling scientists to determine the exact age of any fossil. Powerful microscopes allow the discovery of bacteria in fossils. Computer imaging technology reveals traces of delicate internal organs, such as the heart of a dinosaur that lived 65 million years ago.

💻📖 RESOURCES

- Lanham, Url N. *The Bone Hunters: The Heroic Age of Paleontology in the American West*. Mineola, NY: Dover, 1992.
- Pascoe, Elaine. *New Dinosaurs: Skeletons in the Sand*. Woodbridge, CT: Blackbirch, 1997. (JUV/YA)
- Schopf, J. William. *Cradle of Life: The Discovery of Earth's Earliest Fossils*. Princeton, NJ: Princeton University, 1999.
- PALEONTOLOGISTS AND FOSSIL HUNTERS.
  http://www.zoomschool.com/subjects/dinosaurs/glossary/Paleontologists.shtml
- FREQUENTLY ASKED QUESTIONS ABOUT PALEONTOLOGY.
  http://www.ucmp.Berkeley.edu/FAQ/faq.html

Foucault, Léon

Physicist: demonstrated Earth's rotation
Born: September 18, 1819, Paris, France
Died: February 11, 1868, Paris, France

 Foucault caused a sensation in 1851 when he performed an experiment that proved Earth's rotation. From the dome of the Pantheon, a building in Paris, he suspended an iron ball at the end of a steel wire 220 feet (67 m) long. A pin attached to the bottom of the ball touched a circular ridge of sand on the floor of the Pantheon. When Foucault set the pendulum swinging, the pin scraped a line in the sand each time the weight passed by. The pendulum never changed direction, but swing after swing the lines drawn in the sand followed different directions—the circle of sand was turning! Since the sand was on the Pantheon's floor, which rested on Earth, Foucault had demonstrated that Earth rotates on its axis.

Foucault also investigated **light**, making one of the earliest accurate measurements

A Foucault pendulum

YEARBOOK: 1852

- Based on his work with pendulums, Foucault invents the gyroscope, an instrument consisting of a wheel and an axle mounted in a frame.
- **Elisha Graves Otis** invents the safety elevator.
- Henri Giffard [French: 1825–1882] builds and flies the first steam-powered dirigible.

of its speed. In 1849, he showed that light moves more slowly through water than through air, thereby confirming the wave nature of light.

 **RESOURCES**

- FOUCAULT'S PENDULUM.
  http://www.si.edu/resource/faq/nmah/pendulum.htm

Franklin, Benjamin

Scientist, inventor, printer, statesman, philosopher: proved lightning is electricity
Born: January 17, 1706, Boston, Massachusetts
Died: April 17, 1790, Philadelphia, Pennsylvania

  Franklin's most famous scientific contributions were in the field of electricity. He began experimenting with electricity in 1746, when scientists believed there were two kinds of electricity—one that attracted,

Notable Quotable

Diligence is the mother of good luck.

Being ignorant is not so much a shame as being unwilling to learn.

—Benjamin Franklin

Benjamin Franklin

another that repelled. Franklin showed that there is only one kind of electricity, which flows from a body that has a positive charge to one that has a negative charge.

In 1752, Franklin made a kite with a small metal rod at its top and a metal key at the bottom of its string. He flew the kite during a thunderstorm. After lightning hit the metal rod Franklin put his hand near the key. A spark jumped

Franklin proved that lightning is a form of electricity.

from the key to Franklin's knuckle, proving he had drawn electricity from the clouds down through the kite to the key. He collected some of the electricity in a device called a Leyden jar and later showed that it behaves exactly like other forms of electricity.

Franklin invented the lightning rod, bifocal glasses, an odometer to keep track of distance traveled, and an efficient iron heating stove today known as the Franklin stove. He was one of the first to chart the Gulf Stream, a current in the Atlantic Ocean.

RESOURCES

- Heilbron, J.L. *Electricity in the 17th and 18th Centuries: A Study in Early Modern Physics.* Mineola, NY: Dover, 1999.
- MORE ABOUT BENJAMIN FRANKLIN.
  http://www.english.udel.edu/lemay/franklin/
  http://www.fi.edu/franklin/rotten.html

Sigmund Freud

Freud, Sigmund

Neurologist: founder of psychoanalysis
Born: May 6, 1856, Freiberg, Moravia (now Píbor, Czech Republic)
Died: September 23, 1939, London, England

 At the beginning of the 20th century Freud revolutionized psychology with his theories about how the human mind works. He discovered that our minds preserve memories in the unconscious—the part of our mental processes that normally does not enter our awareness. Many of these memories, he said, are things we repress, such as traumatic events during childhood. Often, he said, these repressed memories surface in dreams.

Freud developed a new method of treating emotional disorders that result from buried memories. Called psychoanalysis, this method is based on people describing their dreams and talking freely about themselves and about anything else that enters their minds. Like Freud, his many followers analyze what patients say, help them uncover past experiences, and lead them toward understanding and dealing with the causes of their problems.

Though Freud's theories have always been controversial, they have had a major impact on millions of individuals as well as on art and other cultural aspects of society.

RESOURCES

- MORE ABOUT SIGMUND FREUD.
  http://www.freud.org.uk/
  http://freud.to.or.at/freud/index-e.htm

Fries, Elias

Botanist: founder of mycology
Born: August 15, 1794, Femsjö, Sweden
Died: February 8, 1878, Uppsala, Sweden

 Even as a boy, Fries was fascinated by mushrooms and other fungi—the study of which is called mycology. As a university student he began to collect and describe as many different species of fungi as possible. This led to his publication of the three-volume *Systema Mycologicum* between 1821 and 1832. In this work, he introduced the first modern system for classifying fungi, based on similarities and differences in the organisms' structure and method of reproduction. Fries also was the first to recognize the close relation between rusts and smuts, two groups of extremely destructive fungi named for the color of their spores (reddish-brown and black, respectively).

Another area of great interest to Fries were lichens, which are composed of two species of organisms, a fungus and an alga, in an association that benefits both (The fungus provides protection and water; the alga supplies food). His system for classifying lichens, presented in 1831, was based on the structure of the reproductive organs. It was widely followed until development of more powerful microscopes led to a better understanding of lichens.

 **RESOURCES**

- MORE ABOUT ELIAS FRIES.

  http://www.systbot.uu.se/dept/history/
  fries.html

  http://www.nrm.se/kbo/saml/fries/
  welcome.html.en

  http://www.biology.au.dk/kursus/mycology/
  HistoryOfMycology/HisFries.htm

Frisch, Karl Von

Zoologist: discovered how bees communicate
Born: November 20, 1886, Vienna, Austria
Died: June 12, 1982, Munich, Germany

 Animal communication is one of the most interesting aspects of **animal behavior**. Frisch found that honeybees communicate the location of food sources using "dance language." A foraging

NOBEL PRIZE 1973

The first Nobel Prize in physiology or medicine awarded for the study of animal behavior went to Frisch, **Nikolaas Tinbergen**, and **Konrad Lorenz**.

bee that returns to the hive and does a circle dance tells other bees that food is close by. To indicate more distant food, the bee does a waggle dance, running along the hive waggling its abdomen from side to

Frisch studied how bees in a colony communicate.

Karl Von Frisch

side. The direction of the waggling run indicates the direction of the food. The slower the dance, the farther the food.

Notable Quotable

The layman may wonder why a biologist is content to devote 50 years of his life to the study of bees and minnows without ever branching out into research on, say, elephants, or at any rate the lice of elephants or the fleas of moles. The answer to any such question must be that every single species of the animal kingdom challenges us with all, or nearly all, the mysteries of life.

—Karl von Frisch

Frisch also disproved the long-held belief that fish and invertebrates are colorblind. For instance, he showed that honeybees can see all colors except red and can even see ultraviolet light. And he trained minnows to respond to colored objects.

 **RESOURCES**

• AUTOBIOGRAPHY OF KARL VON FRISCH.
http://www.nobel.se/medicine/laureates/1973/frisch-autobio.html

Fuel Cells

 Almost every physical process can be completely reversed. Scientists since 1800 have used electric current to break water into hydrogen and oxygen, a process called electrolysis. In 1839, William Robert Grove [British: 1811–1896] reversed the process, obtaining electric

Robert Grove

How It Works

Hydrogen is formed from simple atoms of one electron orbiting one proton. In the basic fuel cell, hydrogen gas flows over a material that takes hydrogen's electron and moves it into a conductor, forming a complete electric circuit. The positively charged proton left behind is attracted to the other end of the circuit, where it re-acquires an electron to become hydrogen again. At the same time, the hydrogen atoms encounter oxygen from the air and combine with it to form water (H_2O), which becomes water-vapor exhaust. Electric power is taken from the fuel cell by attaching a motor or other device to the circuit between the two ends.

current by chemically combining hydrogen and oxygen. A unit called a cell (such as the familiar dry cell) in a chemical battery produces current, and in Grove's device, known as a fuel cell, the cell produces current as long as it is supplied with fuel.

Fuel cells could be ideal power sources, since their only product besides electricity is environmentally benign water, but success has been elusive. One problem is the difficulty of handling hydrogen gas. Obtaining hydrogen from a chemical such as methanol produces environmentally harmful wastes and less energy. Since most fuel cells operate at high temperatures, they can explode, as happened on the ill-fated 1970 *Apollo* XIII mission to the moon.

RESOURCES
• MORE ABOUT FUEL CELLS.

http://www.fuelcells.org/

Fuller, Buckminster

Inventor: developed the geodesic dome
Born: July 12, 1895, Milton, Massachusetts
Died: July 1, 1983, Los Angeles, California

 Fuller was a largely self-educated inventor and architect, whose methods for saving resources made him an early environmentalist. He was always concerned with obtaining the maximum use from the least input. His first major invention, in 1927, named the Dymaxion house, was an inexpensive dwelling suspended from a single mast. In 1933 he created and manufactured a Dymaxion automobile with 3 wheels, designed to use less energy than other transportation. Neither idea was a commercial success although both achieved the goals he set.

A geodesic dome

Fuller's greatest fame comes from his invention of a lightweight, rigid frame for large domes. These are called geodesic domes because the frame, composed of triangular or polygonal facets created by many short, straight segments, repeatedly approximates the geodesic, or shortest distance between two points, along a sphere. The first geodesic dome was shown publicly in 1954 and by 1967 one was used to house the U.S. exhibit at the Montreal World's Fair. Today geodesic domes are popular, especially at scientific research sites, throughout the world.

See also buckyballs.

RESOURCES

- Baldwin, J. *Bucky Works: Buckminster Fuller's Ideas for Today.* New York: John Wiley, 1997.
- Pawley, Martin. *Buckminster Fuller.* Jersey City, NJ: Parkwest, 1991.
- Sieden, Lloyd Steven. *Buckminster Fuller's Universe: His Life and Work.* Cambridge, MA: Perseus, 2000.
- MORE ABOUT BUCKMINSTER FULLER.
  http://www.bfi.org/basic_biography.htm
  http://www.worldtrans.org/whole/bucky.html
  http://www.thirteen.org/cgi-bin/bucky-bin/bucky.cgi

Gabor, Dennis

Physicist: invented holography
Born: June 5, 1900, Budapest, Hungary
Died: February 1979, London, England

 In 1947, Gabor was trying to improve early electron microscopes, which had lenses that were difficult to focus. While sitting on a bench at a tennis club, Gabor conceived of a way to split a beam of electrons to make an image without lenses. These images, which he called holograms (from Greek for "completely written"), could capture all the information and display the result in three dimensions. His early holographic images were unsatis-

Dennis Gabor

factory because he could not control the light well enough. This problem was solved with the invention of the **laser** in 1960, and scientists soon used lasers to make excellent holograms. Gabor's later work

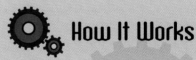

How It Works

To make a hologram, a laser beam is split in two. One part is aimed at the object and reflected onto a photographic plate. The other part is focused directly on the photographic plate. When the two parts meet, they create an interference pattern that is recorded. When this pattern is exposed to another laser beam of the same frequency, a photograph of the object appears in space behind the plate and can be viewed from different angles.

NOBEL PRIZE 1971

Gabor received the Nobel Prize in physics for his invention of holography.

included showing that holograms could be used to record and access large amounts of computer data almost instantaneously.

Gabor's interest in science developed in childhood, as he and his brother built a little laboratory in their home and reproduced experiments they read about. Gabor studied at universities in Budapest and Berlin, then worked at the German company Siemens and Halske, where he invented the quartz mercury lamp. When Adolf Hitler came to power in 1933, Gabor lost his job. He returned to Hungary and in 1934 moved to England.

 **RESOURCES**

- AUTOBIOGRAPHY OF DENNIS GABOR.
  http://www.nobel.se/laureates/
  physics-1971-1-autobio.html
- HOLOGRAPHY COLLECTION.
  http://web.mit.edu/museum/collections/
  holography.html

Galaxies

PTOLEMY (catalogued heavens) ➤ GALILEO (observed Milky Way) ➤ HERSCHEL (nebulas) ➤ Parsons (built large telescope, observed spirals) ➤ Huggins (light from spirals matches stars) ➤ LEAVITT (measured distances to stars) ➤ HUBBLE (spirals outside Milky Way; identified 3 classes)

Galaxies are collections of billions of stars, but they are so far away that most are invisible from Earth without telescopes. A few can be seen from Earth as tiny patches of light.

A spiral galaxy

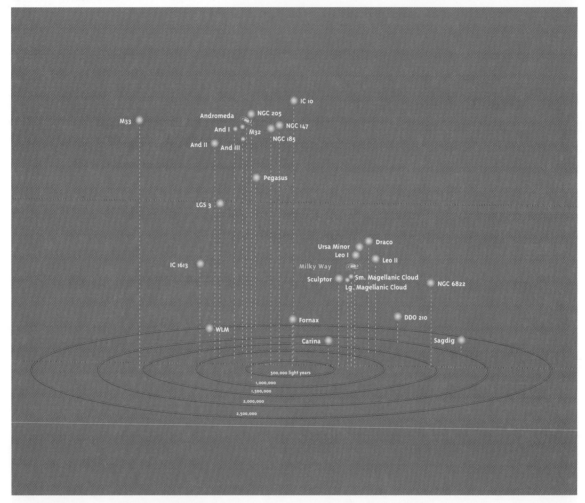

The Milky Way is part of a cluster of galaxies called the Local Group.

The history of galaxy discovery is also the history of advances in the telescope. About 150 C.E., **Claudius Ptolemy** catalogued the heavens as seen with the unaided eye, listing several patches of "misty" light in the sky. After inventing the astronomical telescope in 1609, **Galileo** observed that the largest misty patch, the Milky Way, consists of millions of stars. In fact, the Milky Way is the galaxy that contains our Sun. **William Herschel** used his much bigger telescope starting in 1783 to study thousands of

misty patches, which are called nebulas (from Latin for "clouds"). Herschel guessed that some "nebulas" might actually be like the Milky Way, islands of stars too far away for his telescope to distinguish individually.

In 1845, William Parsons, the Earl of Rosse [English: 1800–1867], built the largest telescope to that date with which he observed that some misty patches have the shape of a spiral. About 20 years later, William Huggins [English: 1824–1910] found that light from one of these spirals, a large patch in Andromeda, matches light emitted by stars and not light emitted by glowing gas, even though the telescope that Huggins used was too weak to detect individual stars.

Astronomers argued over whether the spirals were part of the Milky Way or farther away. In 1908, **Henrietta Leavitt** found a new way to measure distances to stars. Her methods showed that 2 large misty patches that good telescopes revealed as collections of stars, the Magellanic Clouds, are outside the Milky Way. **Edwin Hubble** in 1924 used Leavitt's method with a new large telescope to show that spirals are far outside the Milky Way. The distant islands of stars, surrounded by vast amounts of empty space, were christened "galaxies," from the Greek name for the Milky Way. Hubble identified three major classes of galaxies: spirals like Andromeda and the Milky Way; irregular galaxies like the Magellanic Clouds; and balls of stars called elliptical galaxies.

Galaxies are linked into groups called clusters, which contain dozens or hundreds of galaxies. The clusters group into large regions of hundreds of clusters, called superclusters. Regions between the superclusters, called voids, have few or no galaxies.

RESOURCES

- Friedman Herbert. *The Astronomer's Universe: Stars, Galaxies, and Cosmos.* New York: W.W. Norton, 1998.
- Weisbacher, Anne. *Galaxies.* Edwina, MN: Abdo & Daughters, 1997. (JUV/YA)
- STUDENTS FOR THE EXPLORATION AND DEVELOPMENT OF SPACE.
  http://www.seds.org/messier/galaxy.html

Galen, Claudius

Physician, anatomist: influenced biology for 1,400 years
Born: c. 130, Pergamon, Asia Minor (now Bergama, Turkey)
Died: c. 200, Pergamon, Asia Minor

 Galen, a Greek, was the major biologist of ancient Rome. He studied medicine and became a famous doctor, treating gladiators, soldiers, and emperors. Many of Galen's ideas about human **anatomy** were based on the ideas of **Hippocrates** and other early Greek anatomists. But he also developed new ideas, based on his treatment of patients and his dissections of animals. He was the first person to take a patient's pulse and use it in diagnosing problems. He identified many muscles and showed that different parts of the spinal cord control different muscles. He demonstrated that severing the spinal cord meant that the part of the body below the cut could not move. He showed that arteries contain blood—not air, as had been believed. But some of Galen's ideas were incorrect, such as believing that the liver is the main organ of the blood system and that pores connect the right and left sides of the heart. Galen wrote hundreds of books. For some 1,400 years after his death, his writings were considered infallible and were the basis of medical education.

 **RESOURCES**

- MORE ABOUT CLAUDIUS GALEN.
  http://www.bbc.co.uk/education/medicine/nonint/prehist/dt/prdtbi3.shtml
  http://www.hsc.virginia.edu/hs-library/historical/antiqua/galen.htm
- THE ROMAN PERIOD.
  http://getnet.com/labores/romans.html

Galileo

Physicist, astronomer: stated laws of falling bodies and inertia, invented astronomical telescope
Born: February 18, 1564, Pisa, Italy
Died: January 8, 1642, Arcetri, Italy

 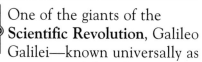 One of the giants of the **Scientific Revolution**, Galileo Galilei—known universally as Galileo—was a principal founder of modern physical science, using careful observation and experimentation to disprove long-held beliefs handed down from the ancient Greeks.

YEARBOOK: 1609

- Galileo builds his first telescope.
- **Johannes Kepler** publishes his theory that planets revolve in elliptical orbits.
- **Tides** in Canada's Bay of Fundy are used as a source of power for the first time.

Galileo made his first famous discovery at age 18, watching an oil lamp swing overhead in wide arcs that gradually turned to narrow arcs. Using his pulse,

Galileo supported Copernicus's theory that the sun is the center of the solar system.

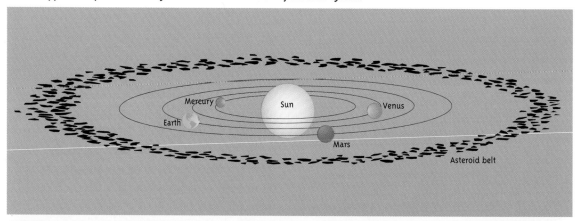

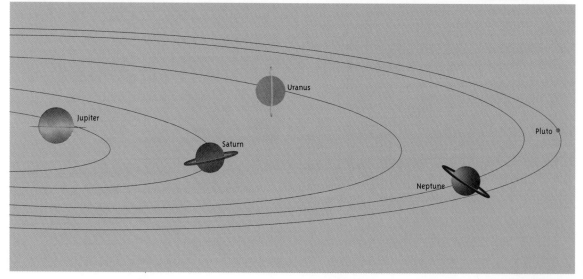

How It Works

Galileo is credited with being the first person to practice a procedure now called the scientific method. This procedure has five basic steps: 1) defining the problem; 2) gathering information related to the problem, through careful observation, reading, and so on; 3) forming a hypothesis, or possible explanation of the problem, based on the information gathered; 4) experimenting to test the hypothesis, using precise measurements and recording all observations; and 5) developing a conclusion based on the experimental data. When sufficient evidence supports the hypothesis, the hypothesis becomes a theory. A theory always is subject to additional testing and revision, and may be changed or discarded over time.

Galileo

he noted that all swings took the same amount of time. He followed this observation with experiments at home and established that a given pendulum always completes its swing in the same time interval, regardless of the arc of the swing.

Notable Quotable

These spots [on the Moon] have never been observed by anyone before me; and from my observations of them, often repeated,...I feel sure that the surface of the Moon is not perfectly smooth, free from inequalities, and exactly spherical, as a large school of philosophers considers with regard to the Moon and the other heavenly bodies, but that, on the contrary, it is full of inequalities, uneven, full of hollows and protuberances, just like the surface of the Earth itself."

—Galileo

Since **Aristotle**, it had been believed that heavy objects fall faster than light ones. According to legend, Galileo disproved this belief in a demonstration at the Leaning Tower of Pisa. From the top of the tower he simultaneously dropped balls of various weights. Observers saw that all the balls hit the ground at the same time.

Galileo reasoned that movement on an inclined plane is similar to that of a body in free fall. Experimenting with ever-steeper inclines, he correctly arrived at the concepts of acceleration and inertia, writing that "any velocity once

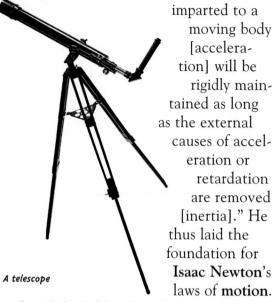

A telescope

imparted to a moving body [acceleration] will be rigidly maintained as long as the external causes of acceleration or retardation are removed [inertia]." He thus laid the foundation for **Isaac Newton**'s laws of **motion**.

In 1609, Galileo heard about a Dutch invention called the **telescope**. He constructed the first of his many telescopes and became the first person to use this instrument to make astronomical discoveries. He observed that the Milky Way galaxy contains a vast quantity of stars "planted together in clusters;" Earth's Moon isn't smooth but has mountains, plains, and craters; and Jupiter has moons revolving around it.

His discovery of Jupiter's four largest moons provided, he believed, a "splendid argument" to support the contention of **Nicolaus Copernicus** that Earth and the other known planets revolve around the sun. For daring to question the belief that Earth is the center of the **universe**, Galileo was threatened with torture, forced to deny his belief in the Copernican system, convicted of challenging the authority of the Roman Catholic Church, and placed under house arrest for the rest of his life.

 RESOURCES
- MacLachlan, James. *Galileo Galilei: First Physicist*. New York: Oxford University, 1999.
- Mitton, Jacqueline. *Galileo: Scientist and Stargazer*. New York: Oxford University, 1998. (JUV/YA)
- Sobel, Dava. *Galileo's Daughter: A Historical Memoir of Science, Faith and Love*. New York: Macmillan, 2000.
- White, Michael. *Galileo Galilei: Inventor, Astronomer, and Rebel*. Woodbridge, CT: Blackbirch Press, 1999. (JUV/YA)
- GALILEO.
  http://galileo.imss.firenze.it/museo/b/egalilg.html

Galton, Francis

Meteorologist, anthropologist: founded eugenics
Born: February 16, 1822, Birmingham, England
Died: January 17, 1911, Haslemere, England

 Galton's long and varied scientific career included important contributions to many fields. He explored parts of Africa; introduced the concept of composite photographs; discovered the rotating wind systems called anticyclones and their effect on weather; and was one of the founders of biometrics (the statistical analysis of biological phenomena). He also developed a mathematical tool for determining how closely related two measurements (such as height and intelligence) might be.

YEARBOOK: 1861
- Galton introduces the modern technique of weather mapping.
- New York and San Francisco are connected by **telegraph**.
- Philipp Reis [German: 1834–1874] transmits musical tones with a device he calls a **telephone**.

Galton is best remembered for his concept of how to influence human evolution. A cousin of **Charles Darwin**, he became interested in heredity following the publication in 1859 of Darwin's *On the Origin of Species*. He accepted Darwin's theory of natural selection and believed that the human species could be improved by encouraging people with exceptional talents to reproduce while discouraging "unfit" people from reproducing. This concept, which Galton called eugenics, had considerable influence in the United States, England, and Germany during the first half of the 20th century but has since been considered racist and lacking in objectivity, and discredited.

RESOURCES

- FRANCIS GALTON.
  http://www.cimm.jcu.edu.au/hist/stats/galton/index.htm

Galvani, Luigi

Physician: studied effects of electricity on living tissue
Born: September 9, 1737, Bologna, Italy
Died: December 4, 1798, Bologna, Italy

In the 1770s Galvani began to experiment with the effects of electricity on animal tissue, especially muscles. He noticed that a dead frog's

Luigi Galvani

muscles twitch when in contact with metals, with a greater reaction occurring when two dissimilar metals, such as brass and iron, are used together. He also got a dead frog's muscles to twitch simply by touching nearby nerves with a pair of scissors during a lightning storm.

Galvani correctly showed that an electric stimulus causes muscle contractions and that nerves conduct electricity. He believed, however, that a frog's tissues contain an electric fluid secreted by the brain, and that he had discovered a previously unknown kind of electricity, animal electricity. His friend **Alessandro Volta** was dubious; he performed his own experiments and explained that the true source of this bodily electricity was a chemical reaction. Galvani's name lives on in terms such as galvanometer (a device for detecting or measuring a small electric current).

RESOURCES

• Heilbron, J.L. *Electricity in the 17th and 18th Centuries: A Study in Early Modern Physics*. Mineola, NY: Dover, 1999.
• Pera, M. *The Ambiguous Frog: The Galvani-Volta Controversy on Animal Electricity*. Princeton, NJ: Princeton University, 1992.

Gears

 Philon (early mention) ➤ Development with water wheels for sawmills ➤ **China** (controls for gear movement)

Gears are simple machines consisting of two or more wheels in contact. Turning one wheel causes the other to rotate in the opposite direction. Interlocking bumps called teeth prevent slippage. If the wheels are different sizes, they vary in their speed of rotation and amount of force. One rotation of a gear with 20 teeth connected to a gear of 5

The gears of a clock

Gears on bicycles allow riders to adjust their speed and effort.

teeth causes 4 rotations—in the opposite direction—of the smaller gear. The force of turning, called torque, also changes between the gears—the torque on the central rotating shaft of the smaller gear is 4 times that on the larger one.

The earliest known mention of gears, around 250 B.C.E., is by Philon [Greek: born c. 300 B.C.E.]. Early gears were used in grain mills and to control related movements in complex instruments; one instrument from about 100 B.C.E., which modeled movements of planets, contained 24 gear wheels. By 400 C.E., gears converted the slow movement of water wheels into speedy rotation for sawmills. Around 720, Chinese inventors developed controls for gear movement that make gravity- and spring-driven **clocks and watches** possible.

Gears are used in nearly all machinery, but are most familiar on bicycles and automobiles. By switching from one size gear to another, torque and speed are adjusted for different tasks.

 RESOURCES

- Glover, David. *Pulleys and Gears*. Westport, CT: Heinemann, 1997. (JUV/YA)
- Good, Keith. *Gear Up: Marvelous Machine Projects*. Minneapolis: Lerner, 2000. (JUV/YA)
- How Stuff Works.

  http://www.howstuffworks.com/gears.htm

Geiger, Hans Wilhelm

Physicist: invented the Geiger counter
Born: September 20, 1882, Neustadt, Germany
Died: September 24, 1945, Potsdam, Germany

 Around 1910, while working with **Ernest Rutherford**, Geiger designed an instrument to detect and measure

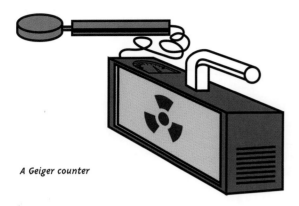

A Geiger counter

radioactivity. He and Walther Müller made an improved version in 1928 and today it is known as the Geiger or Geiger-Müller counter.

Geiger used his counter to help Rutherford establish that an alpha

How It Works

The Geiger counter consists of a metal cylinder filled with gas. A thin wire runs from one end of the cylinder to the other. This wire and the metal wall act as electrodes. When radiation enters the cylinder and collides with a gas atom, the atom becomes ionized (loses one or more electrons). As more and more atoms are ionized, many electrons spread along the wire, creating an electric pulse that can be counted by a meter.

particle is identical to the positively charged nucleus of a helium atom. Another experiment by Geiger led to Rutherford's conclusion that every atom has a positively charged nucleus that repels alpha particles (because like charges repel one another). Today, in addition to scientific studies of radioactive substances, Geiger counters are used by prospectors to find uranium and other radioactive elements.

 **RESOURCES**

- THE GEIGER COUNTER.
  http://www-spof.gsfc.nasa.gov/Education/wgeiger.html
- THE HISTORY OF COSMIC RAY RESEARCH.
  http://www.thomson.u-net.com/CR.htm

Gell-Mann, Murray

Physicist: proposed existence of quarks
Born: September 15, 1929, New York, New York

 Since ancient times, people have tried to discover if the same basic building blocks make up all matter. The problem appeared to be solved in the 19th century when **John Dalton** said that

Murray Gell-Mann

all matter is composed of **atoms**. But during the 20th century dozens of **subatomic particles** were discovered. In 1964, Gell-Mann proposed that heavy subatomic particles are made up of still more basic particles, which he called quarks. He suggested three kinds of quarks, called up, down, and strange. From 1974 to 1984 scientists detected evidence of three additional kinds, called charm, top, and bottom. Today, the quark theory is widely accepted.

NOBEL PRIZE 1969

Gell-Mann was awarded the Nobel Prize in physics for his contributions and discoveries concerning the classification of elementary particles and their interactions.

Gell-Mann's brilliance was apparent at an early age. He entered college at age 15 and at 21 received his Ph.D. Gell-Mann's first major contribution, introduced in 1953, was the concept of strangeness, which explains why heavy subatomic particles decay to lighter particles at slower-than-expected rates. He then developed a new system of classifying heavy particles, called the eightfold way.

 RESOURCES

- Gell-Mann, Murray. *The Quark and the Jaguar: Adventures in the Simple and the Complex.* New York: W.H. Freeman, 1994.
- Johnson, George. *Strange Beauty: Murray Gell-Mann and the Revolution in Twentieth-Century Physics.* New York: Alfred A. Knopf, 1999.
- MURRAY GELL-MANN HOME PAGE.

  http://www.santafe.edu/sfi/People/mgm/

Generators

 OERSTED (current moves magnet) ➤ **HENRY/ FARADAY** (Oersted's effect is reversible) ➤ Gramme (first succesfful generator) ➤ **TESLA** (alternating current)

 Electric motors, lamps, and telegraphs operate on current electricity. Current from chemical batteries became available in 1800. An experiment in 1820 by **Hans Oersted** demonstrated that electric current moves a small magnet. In 1831, **Joseph Henry** in the United States and **Michael Faraday** in England independently recognized that Oersted's effect is reversible: a moving magnet produces current in a nearby conductor. Devices that create current this way are called generators or dynamos. The first inventor to produce a fully successful generator was Zénobe Gramme [Belgian: 1826–1901], who developed the basic model in 1867 and introduced a working version in 1871.

How It Works

A small generator with rotating permanent magnets is used to make an iron wheel into an electromagnet. As the electromagnetic wheel turns, its magnetic field induces current in its container, built with many loops of conducting wire. Current is produced where magnetic field lines travel through the wire.

By 1871, several devices based on current electricity, including the **telegraph**, were already in use. After electric **lighting** was introduced in 1879, companies built large-scale generators and wired entire

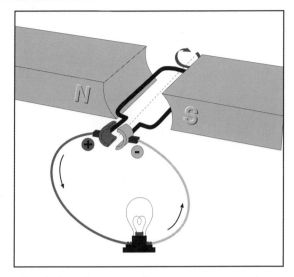

When the loop of wire turns, electric current is generated.

cities, starting as early as 1882. **Nikola Tesla,** in 1883, developed a new type of generator, which produces alternating current (AC). AC can travel long distances at high power and then be transformed to useful levels. The first AC generating plant began operation in 1886. This system remains in common use.

A generator

 **RESOURCES**
• THE HISTORY OF ELECTRICITY.
http://www.scholzelectrical.com.au/electricity.htm

Genes

MENDEL (characteristics controlled by heredity) ➤ **Sutton** (chromosomes) ➤ **MORGAN** (mutations; first chromosome map) ➤ **AVERY** (genes composed of DNA) ➤ **NIRENBERG** (genes as blueprints for proteins) ➤ Researchers decode full genomes

 The science of genetics was born in 1865, when **Gregor Mendel** demonstrated that an organism's characteristics are controlled by hereditary factors, and that these factors occur in pairs. Mendel's report, published in 1866, lay unnoticed by the scientific world until 1900, when scientists working independently in three countries reached similar conclusions—and discovered that Mendel had beaten them by more than 3 decades.

The next questions to be answered were: What are these hereditary factors, where are they located, and how do they work? Answering these questions was one of the greatest achievements of 20th-century biology.

FAMOUS FIRST

In 2000, a 4-year effort to sequence the first complete genome of a flowering plant was concluded by scientists from the United States, Europe, and Japan. The plant, *Arabidopsis thaliana*, is a mustard commonly called thale cress. Its 5 pairs of chromosomes contain a total of 25,498 genes.

Identical twins develop from the same fertilized egg and therefore share the same genes.

In 1902, Walter Sutton [American: 1877–1916] observed the remarkable similarity between Mendel's hereditary factors and **chromosomes**, and proposed that chromosomes carry the hereditary material. By 1911, **Thomas Hunt Morgan** confirmed Sutton's hypothesis and discovered that **mutations** (changes) in the hereditary material occur from time to time. Meanwhile, people began calling the hereditary factors "genes," a term proposed by Wilhelm Johannsen [Danish: 1857–1927] in 1909.

Understanding the molecular structure of genes began in 1944, when **Oswald Theodore Avery** and his colleagues demonstrated that bacteria genes are composed of a nucleic acid they named **DNA**. Other scientists later showed that the genes of almost all organisms consist of DNA (the exceptions are certain viruses, whose genes consist of a related substance called RNA). In addition, the chemical composition and the shape of DNA molecules were determined. Then in 1961, **Marshall Nirenberg** and others showed how genes act as blueprints for the production of **proteins**.

The first chromosome map, showing the location of 5 genes on a fruit fly chromo-

In sexual reproduction, an offspring receives half its genes from its mother and half from its father.

some, was drawn by Morgan in 1911. Through the decades, ever more detailed maps were produced for an ever greater variety of species. For example, the locations of human genes for more than 1,200 inherited disorders have been pinpointed. As the 21st century began, researchers had succeeded in decoding the full sequence of several species' DNA—that is, all the genetic instructions on a species' chromosomes. This sequence is called a genome. Of particular interest to many people is the **Human Genome Project**, which attempts to map all chromosomes of the human body.

There is much genetic similarly among species. Humans and chimpanzees share about 98% of their genes. Fruit flies have similar genes to 68% of genes involved in human cancers.

 **RESOURCES**

- Coen, Enrico. *The Art of Genes: How Organisms Make Themselves.* New York: Oxford University, 2000.
- FROM DARWIN TO THE HUMAN GENOME PROJECT.
  http://www.csuchico.edu/anth/CASP/ Carmosino_P.html
- LANDMARKS IN THE HISTORY OF GENETICS.
  http://members.tripod.com/dorakmt/ genetics/notes01.html

Genetic Engineering

 Cohen/Boyer (transfer of DNA between organisms) ➤ Development of recombination ➤ Development of gene therapy

  Genetic engineering was born in the early 1970s when Stanley Cohen [American: 1922–] and

FAMOUS FIRST

The first human gene therapy occurred in 1990 when a 4-year-old girl received a blood transfusion containing billions of cells with copies of a gene she lacked. The gene enabled her body to make adenosine deaminase, an enzyme essential for a healthy immune system.

 **How It Works**

Cohen and Boyer used **enzymes** called restriction endonucleases to cut a DNA molecule from the bacterium *Escherichia coli* at specific sites. They used other restriction endonucleases to separate certain genes from the DNA molecules of an African clawed toad. They mixed the toad genes with the bacterial DNA and used the enzyme ligase to "glue" the material together. The result was a DNA molecule that was part bacterial and part toad. When this was inserted into normal *Escherichia*, it became part of their genetic structure. When the *Escherichia* reproduced by dividing in half, each offspring inherited the toad genes.

Herbert Boyer [American: 1936–] invented a comparatively simple technique for transferring **DNA** from one species of organism to another. Although genetic engineering includes any deliberate alteration of an organism's genetic material, the term most commonly refers to the process initiated by Cohen and Boyer, now called recombination.

Recombination makes it possible to transfer genes between all kinds of organisms. For example, the human gene that directs production of the hormone insulin can be inserted into the DNA of bacteria. The bacteria and all their descendants then manufacture human insulin. Recombination also makes it possible to transfer normal genes

Genetic engineering techniques introduce new genes into an organism.

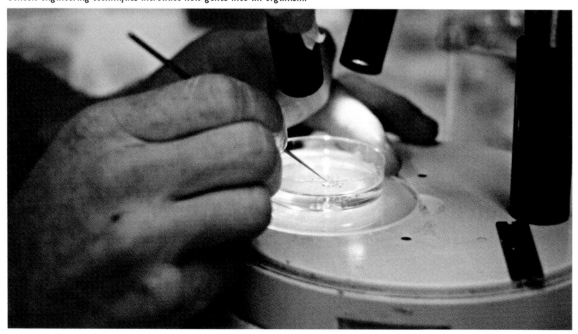

into the cells of people who suffer from diseases caused by defective genes—a procedure known as gene therapy.

Genetic engineering has raised ethical concerns and is controversial, particularly in the areas of **cloning** and genetically modified crops.

RESOURCES

* Bryan, Jenny. *Genetic Engineering.* Austin, TX: Raintree Steck-Vaughn, 1997. (JUV/YA)
* Stanley, Debbie. *Genetic Engineering: The Cloning Debate.* New York: Rosen, 2000.
* Yount, Lisa. *Biotechnology and Genetic Engineering.* New York: Facts on File, 2000.
* TIKI'S GUIDE TO GENETIC ENGINEERING.

http://www.oneworld.org/penguin/genetics/home.html

Geological Time Scale

STENO (strata as ages; fossils are extinct organisms) ➤ **Hutton** (changes as slow natural process) ➤ **Smith** (different strata, different fossils) ➤ **Lyell** (calculated fossil record)

Ancient people believed that the past was like the present—with exceptions. Greeks turned **fossils** into mythological creatures, the Chinese collected bones of "dragons," and various cultures spoke of giants who once terrorized Earth. In 1667, **Nicolaus Steno** proposed that rock layers, called strata, represent different ages and that fossils are remains of extinct living creatures from those ages. Steno pictured great catastrophes ending a half dozen such ages, but in 1788, James Hutton [Scottish:

The immensity of geological time is measured in eons, eras, periods, and epochs. In the diagram, a tiny slice of time from one timeline is expanded in the timeline to its right.

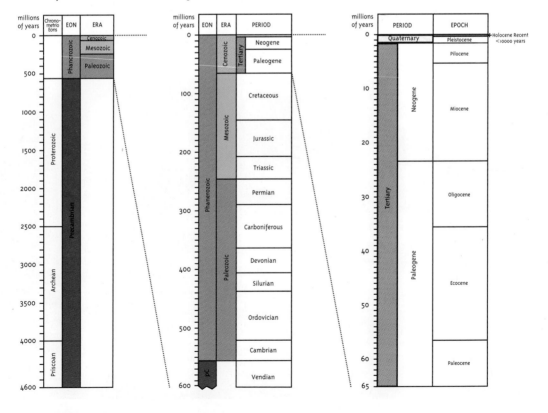

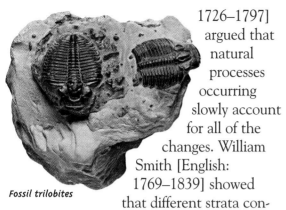

Fossil trilobites

1726–1797] argued that natural processes occurring slowly account for all of the changes. William Smith [English: 1769–1839] showed that different strata contain different fossils but that the same strata and fossils could be found all over England. In the 1830s, Charles Lyell [Scottish: 1797–1875] convinced many scientists that Hutton and Smith had been correct but astonished scientists by calculating that the fossil record covers 240 million years—vastly longer than the 5 or 6 thousand years that most expected. Today's scientists, however, using radioactive **dating**, know that it is much longer yet—almost 4 billion years.

Many geologists contributed to separating the geological record into a series of eons, eras, periods, and epochs, beginning about 1790. The periods were identified by their characteristics, such as Carboniferous for coal-bearing and Cretaceous for chalky; by sequence, such as Eocene (dawn period); by peoples, such as Cambrian for early inhabitants of Wales; or by places, such as Jurassic for the Jura Mountains of Europe. By 1840, most of the names has been assigned, although a few were added in the 1870s.

RESOURCES

- More about the Geologic Time Scale.
- http://www.geo.ucalgary.ca/macrae/timescale/timescale.html
- http://www.ucmp.berkeley.edu/exhibit/histgeoscale.html

Gibbon, John H.

Surgeon: invented heart-lung machine
Born: September 29, 1903, Philadelphia, Pennsylvania
Died: February 5, 1973, Media, Pennsylvania

 Before Gibbon invented the heart-lung machine, it was not possible to do open-heart surgery. The heart could not be stopped for more than a minute or two; anything longer and the brain and other organs would begin to die from a lack of oxygen.

In the 1930s, Gibbon set about developing a pump that would maintain blood circulation during heart surgery. After various redesigns he produced a machine

John Gibbon

that shunted the blood away from the heart, efficiently added oxygen to it, and returned it to the body. Gibbon successfully tested the machine on animals, and then on May 6, 1953, used it on a human for the first time; the machine completely took over the work of the heart and lungs for 29 minutes while a heart defect in an 18-year-old woman was repaired.

RESOURCES

• Dr. John H. Gibbon's Life and Career.
http://www.mc.vanderbilt.edu/cvpt/gibbon.htm

• Short History of Heart Valve Surgery.
http://heart-surgeon.com/history.html

Glass

Glass was among the first materials used by early humans, who flaked natural glass, called obsidian, into sharp-edged tools. Obsidian occurs when melted rock from a volcano cools quickly. All glass behaves like liquid that has suddenly turned solid.

More than 5,000 years ago, potters discovered that some high-temperature **ceramics** develop a thin coat of glass (a glaze). By about 4,000 years ago,

A glass blower

Stained glass

in windows. Reinforcing glass with wire mesh (1893) or a layer of **plastic** (1905) helped keep windows from shattering, especially important for vehicle windows.

Since 1942, glass fibers have been used for insulation and to strengthen plastics. More recently they have become the basis of **fiber optics**.

 RESOURCES

- Fisher, Leonard Everett. *The Glassmakers* (Colonial Craftsmen). Tarrytown, NY: Benchmark, 1997. (JUV/YA)
- Houston, James. *Fire into Ice: Adventures in Glass Making*. Toronto: Tundra, 1998.
- More about Glass.

  http://www.cmog.org/

  http://www.civilization.ca/membrs/canhist/verre/veintooe.html

Glidden, Joseph

Farmer: invented barbed wire
Born: January 18, 1813, Charlestown, New Hampshire
Died: October 9, 1906, De Kalb, Illinois

 When homesteaders began settling the Great Plains of North America they wanted to fence their land. Materials used to build fences elsewhere, such as rocks and lumber, were scarce. Shrubs and hedges took too long to grow.

experiments or accidents revealed that sand and the mineral sodium carbonate when heated together melt into liquid glass that can be cast in molds. For the next 2,000 years or so, glass objects were cast or shaped by cutting, a slow, difficult process. About 50 B.C.E. the invention in Lebanon of glassblowing made it possible to produce glass objects rapidly. Glass became more common and was soon used

FAMOUS FIRST

In 1912, the Corning Glass Works developed the first glass that does not shatter when quickly heated or cooled. After a worker's wife used the new glass to bake a cake for the staff, Corning began in 1915 to manufacture glass cookware, called Pyrex.

YEARBOOK: 1874

- Glidden patents his barbed wire.
- German chemist Othmar Zeidler is first to synthesize DDT.
- Willy Kuhne [German: 1837–1900] discovers the **enzyme** trypsin.
- English pharmacist C.R. Alder Wright synthesizes heroin for the first time.

Barbed wire fencing

Strands of smooth wire were easily broken by cattle. In the 1860s inventors tried adding points to smooth wire. One created the "thorny fence," a double-strand design with sharp points.

In the early 1870s, Glidden saw someone demonstrate a cattle deterrent consisting of a double fence: a line of smooth wire and, inside it, a wood rail with protruding nails. This inspired Glidden to invent the barbed wire we know today, in which one wire is twisted around another in such a way that the barbs are locked in place. Glidden also designed machinery to mass-produce his invention, which quickly led to the wire's widespread use. Today, in addition to fencing in farms and ranches, barbed wire is used to protect military

camps, warehouses, construction sites, and other property.

 **RESOURCES**

- MORE ABOUT BARBED WIRE.

  http://www.barbwiremuseum.com/barbedwirehistory.htm

  http://www.nara.gov/education/teaching/glidden/wire.html

Gliders

CAYLEY (first glider) ➤ **Lilienthal** (steered glider) ➤ **WRIGHT BROTHERS** (airplane)

 Gliders are similar to parachutes and kites—they use motion through air to provide lift. But unlike parachutes, gliders can be guided easily to places where air lifts them higher; and unlike kites, no tether is needed.

The first person to build a glider was **George Cayley**, in 1808. He studied bird wings and recognized that soaring uses the curved top of wings. As air moves over curved wings, it travels faster above the wing than below. This lowers air pressure above the wing, which is then pushed up by the denser air below. Cayley's 1853 glider, with three sets of wings, carried a man during a short flight. In 1871, Otto Lilienthal [German: 1848–1896] continued Cayley's work. By 1877, Lilienthal developed a glider launched by running down a hill and steered by positioning his legs. By 1895, working with his brother, he produced the first glider that soared higher than the point of takeoff.

Other aviation pioneers used gliders as a step in the development of the airplane, including the **Wright brothers** in 1901.

After the German defeat in World War I (1918), Germans were forbidden to build airplanes, so they developed improved gliders. Both sides employed gliders in some World War II battles.

Gliding today is a sport. Gliders resembling engineless airplanes may be towed by airplanes and launched high in the sky. Small tetherless kites called hang gliders, launched from cliffs or car tows, are very popular. The pilot is suspended from the kite as it flies and and steers by shifting body position.

 RESOURCES

- Jennings, Terry. *Planes, Gliders, Helicopters, and other Flying Machines*. London: Kingfisher, 1993.(JUV/YA)
- Whelan, Robert F. *Cloud Dancing: Your Introduction to Gliding and Motorless Flight*. Highland City, FL: Rainbow, 1996.
- More about Gliders.

  http://wings.ucdavis.edu/Book/Vehicles/beginner/gliders-01.html

A modern glider

Glisson, Francis

Physician: described rickets
Born: 1597, Rampisham, England
Died: October 16, 1677, London, England

Rickets is a childhood disease characterized by deformed bones. The first medical description was made by Daniel Whistler [English: 1619–1684] in 1645. During the next few years Glisson and some of his friends studied rickets—an early example of researchers working together—and in 1651 Glisson published an excellent account of the disease. He did not, however, know the cause of rickets. It wasn't until the 20th century that scientists determined that rickets is caused by a deficiency of **vitamin** D.

In 1654, Glisson published a detailed description of healthy and diseased livers. In 1672 he proposed that all living tissues have the ability to contract when stimulated, a property he called "irritability." Several years later he noted that when a muscle contracts it does not change in volume. Glisson's writings on "irritability" influenced the work of **Albrecht von Haller.**

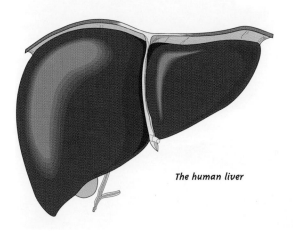

The human liver

 **RESOURCES**

• HISTORY OF VITAMIN D.
  http://vitamind.ucr.edu/history.html

Global Warming

Tyndall (atmospheric gases warm Earth) ➤
Arrhenius (carbon dioxide traps heat) ➤
Revelle/Suess (consequences of warming)

In 1861, John Tyndall [Irish: 1820–1893] suggested that gases in the **atmosphere** keep Earth warm. This was confirmed in 1896, when Svante Arrhenius [Swedish: 1859–1927] discovered that atmospheric carbon dioxide traps enough reflected heat to warm Earth's surface.

Since the **Industrial Revolution,** people have been pouring ever-increasing amounts of carbon dioxide and other heat-trapping gases into the atmosphere. In 1957, Roger Revelle [American: 1907–1991] and Hans Suess [Austrian-American: 1875–1989] warned that humans were conducting a massive experiment with unpredictable consequences. At their urging, scientists began modern carbon dioxide monitoring programs, which have confirmed that atmospheric carbon dioxide concentrations are increasing. Combined with measurements of carbon dioxide in air trapped in glacial ice, it is evident that in the past 100 years carbon dioxide concentrations have increased more than 25 percent.

Earth's average surface temperature increased about 1° F (0.5° C) during the 20th century, with the greatest increase in recent decades. Leading scientists predict that, within the next few decades, Earth will be warmer than at any time in

Above: *Dry lake bed*
Below: *Automobile emissions contribute to global warming*

the past 1,000 years. By the middle of the 21st century, it may be warmer than at any time in the past 125,000 years. Scientists believe this global warming will have a major impact on climate, glaciers, sea levels, ecosystems, the spread of disease, and agriculture.

See also pollution controls.

 RESOURCES

- Christianson, Gale E. *Greenhouse, The 200-Year Story of Global Warming*. New York: Viking Penguin, 2000.
- Houghton, John T. *Global Warming: The Complete Briefing*. New York: Cambridge University, 1997.
- Tesar, Jenny. *Global Warming*. New York: Facts on File, 1991. (JUV/YA)
- MORE ABOUT GLOBAL WARMING.

  http://www.ncdc.noaa.gov/ol/climate/
  globalwarming.html

  http://www.microtech.com.au/daly/
  bull120.htm

Glomar Challenger Mission

Began: August 11, 1968
Ended: November 11, 1983

 Today the idea that new oceans continually form as a result of **plate tectonics** is accepted as absolute fact. But in 1968, when the ocean-drilling ship *Glomar Challenger* began operations, the theory of plate tectonics was only 4 years old and still controversial. The *Glomar Challenger* drilled and raised long columns, known as cores, from the ocean's bottom. The cores were dated and magnetic orientations established, providing definite proof of sea-floor spreading, a major hypothesis of plate tectonics.

Each separate trip of the *Glomar Challenger's* 15-year mission was called a leg. During the 96 legs, 624 different sites were drilled and 19,119 cores recovered. More than 60 miles (97 km) of cores were brought back for examination. The ship drilled in water as deep as 4.38 miles (7.04 km) and more than a mile (1.61 km) into the ocean floor. It circumnavigated the Earth 13 times.

Some of the most dramatic finds were potential new sources of oil beneath the sea, now one of the main sources of petroleum. Cores confirmed the worldwide layer of debris that marked the collision thought to have caused dinosaur extinction. Today the ocean drilling program continues with newer ships, but *Glomar Challenger* was the pioneer.

RESOURCES

- Hsu, Kenneth J. *Challenger at Sea.* Princeton, NJ: Princeton University, 1992.
- More about Ocean Drilling.

  http://www-odp.tamu.edu/glomar.html

  http://pubs.usgs.gov/publications/text/glomar.html

Tectonic plates form Earth's surface

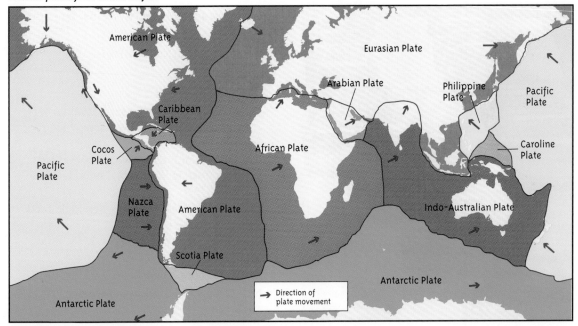

Goddard, Robert Hutchings

Rocket scientist: launched first liquid-propellant rocket
Born: October 5, 1882, Worcester, Massachusetts
Died: August 10, 1945, Baltimore, Maryland

 As a teenager Goddard became enthralled by **rockets** and the possibility of space travel. He spent the rest of his life developing ever-more sophisticated rockets and demonstrating the feasibility of using rockets to reach what he called "extreme altitudes."

FAMOUS FIRST

Goddard's first paper, "A Method of Reaching Extreme Altitudes," was published in 1919. In it, Goddard explained that rockets could carry scientific instruments into space and suggested that it would be possible to reach the Moon using a multistage rocket. The first stage, to launch the vehicle, would be the most powerful. Each succeeding stage would be less powerful because the vehicle would face less and less resistance as it climbed out of Earth's atmosphere.

Goddard's early work was with solid-fuel rockets. In 1914 he received the first of 214 patents, for a 2-stage powder rocket. Goddard began researching liquid fuels, which are more energy efficient, in

Notable Quotable

What sunbound astronaut's experience can equal that of Robert Goddard, whose body stayed on Earth while he voyaged through galaxies?

Charles A. Lindbergh

Robert Goddard and one of his early rockets

1921. On March 16, 1926, he launched the world's first liquid-propellant rocket from a hill in Massachusetts. It reached an altitude of 41 feet (12.5 m). Three years later, he launched a rocket that reached an altitude twice as high. Frightened neighbors complained and local officials banned further launches. Goddard moved his work to the New

Goddard laid groundwork for the space shuttle program.

Mexico desert, where he developed rockets that reached speeds over 700 miles per hour (1,100 kph) and estimated altitudes over 8,000 feet (2,500 m).

Goddard demonstrated that rockets operate better in a vacuum than in air. He devised ways to obtain a continuous flow of power and to cool the combustion chamber. He invented guidance mechanisms for steering rockets during their ascent and used parachutes for their descent.

 **RESOURCES**

• Streissguth, Thomas. *Rocket Man: The Story of Robert Goddard*. Minneapolis: Carolrhoda, 1995. (JUV/YA)

• ROBERT HUTCHINGS GODDARD.
  http://www.spaceline.org/history/22.html

Goldmark, Peter

Engineer: developed first color television system, 33 1/3 LP recording
Born: December 2, 1906, Budapest, Hungary
Died: December 7, 1977, Westchester County, New York

 Goldmark—who helped revolutionize the **television** and **sound recording** industries—emigrated to the United States in 1933 and in 1936 joined the Columbia Broadcasting System (CBS). There he led development of the first practical color television system, which used a rotating 3-color disk with filters for red, green, and blue. He first demonstrated it in 1940. It was not compatible with black-and-white sets and was superseded by an all-electronic system.

In 1948, Columbia introduced the 33⅓-rpm phonograph record, created by Goldmark. Called the LP, for "long playing," it had a much narrower groove than the popular 78-rpm records. This enabled one LP to hold the equivalent of 6 78s.

Goldmark also developed a scanning system that was used by the U.S. Lunar Orbiter in 1966 to relay photographs to Earth from the Moon. And he developed the first electronic video recording system, a forerunner of today's VCRs.

Early television set

RESOURCES

- INVENTING TELEVISION.

  http://www.inventorsmuseum.com/
  television.htm

- RECORDING TECHNOLOGY HISTORY.

  http://history.acusd.edu/gen/recording/
  notes.html

Golgi, Camillo

Physician: developed stain for nervous tissue
Born: July 7, 1844, Corteno, Italy
Died: January 21, 1926, Pavia, Italy

 Under a microscope, a thin slice of living tissue appears colorless. Adding a stain can color some parts but not others, creating a contrast that helps researchers see details more clearly. In 1873, Golgi developed a method of staining nervous tissue with a silver compound, revolutionizing the study of neurons (nerve cells). Golgi was able to show all the regions of a neuron and identify the two main kinds: neurons with long axons (filaments) that extend outside the central nervous system and neurons with short axons that remain within the central nervous system.

NOBEL PRIZE 1906

The Nobel Prize in physiology or medicine was awarded to Golgi and *Santiago Ramón y Cajal* for their work on the structure of the nervous system.

The stain also allows better study of the interior of neurons. In 1898, Golgi reported the presence near the nucleus of a structure consisting of a stack of flat sacs. The existence of this organelle—now called the Golgi apparatus—was debated for many years; it wasn't until the 1950s and the advent of powerful electron microscopes that its existence was verified, not only in neurons but in most kinds of cells.

Golgi also studied malaria, building on work by **Charles Louis Alphonse Laveran** and others. Golgi showed that the release of the malarial parasite from the liver into a patient's blood is related to the onset of fever, and observed the effectiveness of quinine in fighting the parasite in different stages of its life cycle.

RESOURCES

- LIFE AND DISCOVERIES OF CAMILLO GOLGI.

  http://www.nobel.se/medicine/articles/golgi/

Goodall, Jane

Animal behaviorist: revolutionized understanding of chimpanzees
Born: April 3, 1934, London, England

 Chimpanzees are humans' closest relatives but before 1960 little was known about their behavior in the wild. The anthropologist **Louis S.B. Leakey** believed that learning about chimpanzees would provide a better understanding of humans and their evolution. Goodall was working for Leakey at Olduvai Gorge, a famous fossil site in what today is Tanzania. She was eager to study living animals, and Leakey encouraged her to set up a camp in

FAMOUS FIRST

In 1991, Goodall started Roots & Shoots, a youth program to promote care and concern for animals and the environment.

Jane Goodall

Chimpanzee

their natural habitat. She discovered that chimpanzees are not vegetarians, as had been believed, but also eat meat and even practice cannibalism. She saw that they develop family relationships and use touch to comfort one another. She watched them use twigs as tools for gathering and eating termites. As Goodall reported her discoveries, it became apparent that humans are not as different from chimpanzees as had been assumed.

nearby Gombe Stream Reserve (now Gombe National Park). From 1960 until 1970, Goodall observed chimpanzees in

Today, Goodall lives in the United States. She still spends time occasionally in Gombe, but much of her work centers on educating people about the importance of protecting wildlife and the environment.

See also animal behavior.

Notable Quotable

I have been interested in animals since before I can remember. When I was four years old, I stayed on a farm where I helped to collect hen's eggs. I became puzzled and asked those around me, "Where is the hole big enough for the eggs to come out?" When no one answered to my satisfaction, I hid in a small, stuffy henhouse for some four hours to find out. When my mother saw me rushing toward the house, she noticed my excitement. Instead of scolding me for disappearing for so long (the family had even called the police!), she sat down and listened to me tell the wonderful story of how a hen lays an egg.

—Jane Goodall

 RESOURCES

- Goodall, Jane. *Jane Goodall—40 Years at Gombe.* New York: Stewart, Tabori & Chang, 1999.
- Goodall, Jane. *My Life with Chimpanzees.* New York: Simon and Schuster, 1988.
- Pettit, Jane. *Jane Goodall, Pioneer Researcher.* Danbury, CT: Franklin Watts, 1999. (JUV/YA)
- Senn, Joyce. *Jane Goodall, Naturalist.* Woodbridge, CT: Blackbirch, 1993. (JUV/YA)
- THE JANE GOODALL INSTITUTE.
  http://www.janegoodall.org/

Goodyear, Charles

Inventor: discovered vulcanization of rubber
Born: December 29, 1800, New Haven, Connecticut
Died: July 1, 1860, New York, New York

 Goodyear was a fanatic about rubber. "There is probably no other inert substance which so excites the mind," he once said. But rubber had limited usefulness in the early 1800s. It became sticky and soft in summer and bone-hard in winter.

Notable Quotable

Life should not be estimated exclusively by the standard of dollars and cents. I am not disposed to complain that I have planted and others have gathered the fruits. A man has cause for regret only when he sows and no one reaps.

—Charles Goodyear

In the 1830s Goodyear began to look for ways to make rubber commercially useful. He conducted his first experiments while in debtors' prison, spending hour after hour kneading raw rubber. After his release, he continued to experiment. He added drying agents, which reduced the stickiness. One day he applied nitric acid to a piece of rubber to remove some paint. The surface of the rubber turned black and smooth, but underneath it remained sticky.

In 1839, Goodyear accidentally dropped some rubber mixed with sulfur on a hot stove. Instead of melting, the rubber became dry and elastic. Goodyear had discovered the process now called vulcanization (Vulcan is the Roman name for the god of fire.) Heating and sulfur strengthened the

Rubber tires

rubber so that it could be used commercially. Goodyear spent the rest of his life promoting rubber, suggesting its use in paint, wheelbarrow tires, inflatable life rafts, and numerous other applications.

 RESOURCES

- CHARLES GOODYEAR AND THE STRANGE STORY OF RUBBER.
  http://www.goodyear.com/us/corporate/strange.html

Gram, Hans Christian

Physician: developed method to stain bacteria
Born: September 13, 1853, Copenhagen, Denmark
Died: November 11, 1938, Copenhagen, Denmark

 Gram built on work done by **Paul Ehrlich** and in 1884 developed a staining technique for bacteria now known as the Gram reaction. First, bacteria are placed on a glass slide and stained with an aniline dye, either crystal violet or gentian violet. The slide is washed briefly in water and covered with an iodine solution for a minute. Then it is immersed in an alcohol solution, which removes the violet color from some bacteria (called Gram negative) but not from others (Gram positive). The Gram negative cells then are stained with safranin, a red dye. The difference in staining results from differences in the composition and structure of the bacteria's cell wall. Being able to separate bacteria into 2 major groups is very useful for identifying, classifying, and combating these organisms; for example, the 2 groups react to different antibiotics.

RESOURCES

• BACTERIAL COLONIES, GRAM REACTION, AND CELL SHAPE.
http://helios.bto.ed.ac.uk/bto/microbes/shape.htm#crest

Gravity

ARISTOTLE (theory of gravity) ➤ GALILEO (all bodies in vacuum fall with same acceleration) ➤ NEWTON (gravity as universal force) ➤ EINSTEIN (theory of gravity, general relativity)

Aristotle explained gravity as a natural tendency of objects to fall toward Earth at a speed that depends on the weight of the object. Although this may seem sensible, it is not correct. **Galileo's** experiments, published in 1638, showed that when air resistance is ignored, all bodies fall to

A falling apple inspired Newton

Gravity causes water to drop over a fall.

Earth with the same acceleration, increasing in distance fallen with the square of time falling. In 1665, **Isaac Newton** recognized that gravity is a universal force extending through space. All pairs of masses are attracted by an amount that increases with the product of the masses and that decreases with the square of the distance between their centers. Newton's law of gravity can be used to show the paths of planets around the Sun as well as to compute the speed of a falling object.

In 1915, **Albert Einstein** published an improved theory of gravity, known as general relativity. According to relativity, an object's mass curves space, and motions of objects follow the curves. Einstein's theory explained mysteries about the orbit of the planet Mercury and successfully predicted a different behavior for light from Newton's theory. It also predicted gravity waves, which are yet to be detected.

 RESOURCES

• Strathern, Paul. *Newton and Gravity* (The Big Idea). New York: Doubleday Anchor, 1998. (JUV/YA)

• MORE ABOUT GRAVITY.
  http://www3.actden.com/sky_den/gravity.htm

Gray, Asa

Botanist: pioneer of plant geography
Born: November 18, 1810, Sauquoit, New York
Died: January 30, 1888, Cambridge, Massachusetts

 In the early 1800s little was known about the plants of North America, particularly those of the west. Gray, often considered the founder of American botany, amassed a large collection of specimens. Some he collected himself; others came from fellow scientists or people exploring new territories. Gray set about classifying and naming the plants. His first paper, written in 1834, was on North American sedges.

Gray's collection also included specimens from Europe and Asia. He helped pioneer the field of plant geography—that is, how species are distributed on Earth's surface.

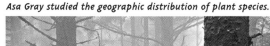
Asa Gray studied the geographic distribution of plant species.

Asa Gray

He compared specimens from various places and deduced that similar species in eastern North America and eastern Asia

FAMOUS FIRST

Gray authored numerous books including, with John Torrey [American: 1796–1873], *A Flora of North America*—the first attempt to describe every kind of plant growing in North America.

had a common ancestor but over time had become distinct. This work influenced **Charles Darwin**. In turn, Gray became a leading U.S. advocate of Darwin's theory of evolution.

RESOURCES
• ASA GRAY (1810–1888).
http://www.nceas.ucsb.edu/alroy/lefa/Gray.html

Gross, Al

Inventor: created the walkie-talkie
Born: 1918, Toronto, Canada
Died: December 21, 2000, Sun City, Arizona

 "Growing up, I fell in love with **radio** technology, but I wanted to take it everywhere with me," recalled Gross. Today's revolution in wireless personal communications began with Gross, who in 1938 invented a device he called the walkie-talkie. It was a portable handheld radio that could transmit and receive messages at short range over land. The U.S. military saw the potential of the device and recruited Gross into the Office of Strategic Services (forerunner of the Central Intelligence Agency). This led to

Walkie-talkies have many applications.

Gross' invention of a 2-way ground-to-air battery-operated communications system that could transmit up to 30 miles (48 km). The system allowed the military to communicate with aircraft and with people behind enemy lines during World War II.

After the war, Gross began producing two-way radios for the general public and pioneered citizens band (CB) radio. He came up with new devices, too. He invented the first wireless pager, technology used in cordless and cellular phones, and a battery-operated unattended weather station. His work inspired cartoonist Chester Gould, who gave his comic strip detective Dick Tracy a 2-way wrist radio after seeing a watch with a built-in beeper and a wireless microphone in Gross' workshop.

 **RESOURCES**

- MORE ABOUT AL GROSS.

  http://web.mit.edu/invent/www/
  inventorsA-H/gross.html

  http://www.spectrum.ieee.org/INST/aug95/
  pph.html

Guericke, Otto von

Physicist: invented air pump
Born: November 20, 1602, Magdeburg, Germany
Died: May 11, 1686, Hamburg, Germany

 Guericke's first major scientific contribution, in 1650, was his invention of a device for removing air from a closed space. Other scientists, notably **Robert Boyle** and **Robert Hooke**, soon used air pumps to study the properties of air.

Eager to try to disprove the long-held belief that it is impossible for a **vacuum** to exist, Guericke constructed a hollow sphere consisting of 2 halves, which came to be called Magdeburg hemispheres for his hometown. Guericke used the hemispheres to demonstrate air pressure and his ability to create a partial vacuum. In a famous experiment in 1654, he showed that 2 teams of 8 horses could not pull apart 2 joined hemispheres after the air within had been removed.

Guericke also built the first apparatus for generating **static electricity**. The friction of his hand rubbing against a rotating ball of sulfur produced sparks, and objects attracted to the rubbed sulfur were repelled once they touched it.

 RESOURCES

- OTTO VON GUERICKE (1602–1686).

  http://www.uni-magdeburg.de/
  magdeburg/guericke_eng.html

- A SHORT HISTORY OF VACUUM TERMINOLOGY AND TECHNOLOGY.

  http://www.mcallister.com/vacuum.html

Guns and Ammunition

 China (first cannon) ➤ **Europe** (hand-carried guns) ➤ **Forsyth** (percussion lock) ➤ **Colt** (revolver) ➤ **Maxim** (machine gun) ➤ Development of automatic and semiautomatic weapons

 Gunpowder, the first **explosive,** was invented more than 400 years before the first firearms —cannons—were developed. The first definite report of a cannon is from China in 1288, followed in 1313 by a German description of an iron barrel used as a cannon and a 1326 European drawing of a small cannon firing arrows. Twenty

A cannon

years later, English soldiers employed 10 cannons in the siege of Calais. After that, cannons were regularly used by all armies and navies. Hand-carried guns, or small arms, were introduced in Europe as early as 1383.

All early small arms and cannons were muzzleloaders, meaning that gunpowder and the projectile were pushed down the barrel from the front. Improvements in muzzleloaders came in the methods of igniting the charge. Early guns used a small pan of powder set under a small hole in the back of the barrel.

When the powder in the pan exploded, its flame shot through the hole and set off the charge in the barrel. In one early mechanism for small arms, pulling a trigger shifted a slow burning match to ignite the pan. Later devices, such as metal wheels and pieces of the hard rock flint, created sparks that set off the pan and fired the gun. The flame-producing mechanism is called a lock, so guns from the 16th through 18th centuries are called match locks, wheel locks, and flintlocks. In 1807, Alexander John Forsyth [Scottish: 1769–1843] invented a device that explodes when struck a sharp blow, called a percussion lock. With the percussion lock, small arms can be loaded from the back of the barrel, called breech loading. By 1846, cartridges were developed that contain the percussion igniter, gunpowder, and bullet in one metal casing, or shell. Some guns called shotguns used special cartridges that fired many small balls (shot) instead of a single bullet.

An improvement from about 1500, still used today, is adding grooves inside a gun's barrel to make the bullet spin, which helps keep its path straight. An old French word for making scratches, as with a file, is "rifler," so the grooves are called rifling and guns with long grooved barrels are called rifles.

Pistols are small arms that can be fired while held by one hand. In 1835, Samuel Colt [American: 1814–1863] invented the revolver, a pistol that rotates a new bullet into position to replace each one fired.

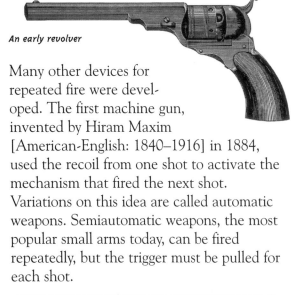

An early revolver

Many other devices for repeated fire were developed. The first machine gun, invented by Hiram Maxim [American-English: 1840–1916] in 1884, used the recoil from one shot to activate the mechanism that fired the next shot. Variations on this idea are called automatic weapons. Semiautomatic weapons, the most popular small arms today, can be fired repeatedly, but the trigger must be pulled for each shot.

 RESOURCES

• Hogg, Ian V. *The Story of the Gun.* 2nd ed. New York: St. Martins, 1996.
• MORE ABOUT GUN HISTORY.

  http://medstat.med.utah.edu/WebPath/ TUTORIAL/GUNS/GUNHIST.html

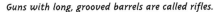

Guns with long, grooved barrels are called rifles.

Gutenberg, Johannes

Printer: invented printing in Europe
Born: c. 1395, Mainz, Germany
Died: February 3, 1468, Mainz, Germany

 As the 15th century dawned in Europe, books were still being copied by hand, a laborious, time-consuming process that made them scarce and expensive. By the time the century ended, the **printing** revolution was underway.

Around 1450, Guttenberg transformed a wine press into a printing press and concocted a smudge-resistant ink from oil, resin, and soap. He became the first European known to mass-produce books and documents.

Until recently, Gutenberg also was credited with inventing the metal mold method of printing—the so-called

Johannes Gutenberg

movable type used by printers until around 1950. This method uses metal molds to create hundreds of identical letters. In 2001, two researchers who had used computers to magnify the type in Gutenberg documents reported that individual letters differed sufficiently to show they could not have come from the same metal molds. The researchers suggested that Gutenberg used a cruder printing method called sand casting, and that someone else invented the metal mold method at a slightly later date.

 RESOURCES

- HISTORY OF THE GUTENBERG BIBLE.
  http://www.gutenbergbible.net/History1.htm
- INVENTING PRINTING.
  http://www.inventorsmuseum.com/Printing.htm

Haber, Fritz

Chemist: synthesized ammonia
Born: December 9, 1868, Breslau, Germany (now Wroclaw, Poland)
Died: January 29, 1934, Basel, Switzerland

 Throughout his scientific career, Haber sought to apply chemistry to the manufacture of useful products. His most important contribution was developing an inexpensive method for making ammonia, a nitrogen-hydrogen compound important in fertilizers and explosives.

NOBEL PRIZE 1918

Haber received the Nobel Prize in chemistry for his synthesis of ammonia.

Fritz Haber

Haber devised a practical, economic process. Carl Bosch [German: 1874–1940] designed the necessary industrial equipment and in 1910 large-scale production of ammonia began. The Haber-Bosch process continues to be the method used to manufacture ammonia.

 RESOURCES

- BIOGRAPHY OF FRITZ HABER.

  http://www.nobel.se/chemistry/laureates/1918/haber-bio.html

By the beginning of the 20th century scientists had made small amounts of ammonia by combining nitrogen gas from the air with hydrogen gas at a temperature of 1832° F (1000° C)— much too high to be practical. Using a catalyst, Haber obtained the same reaction at 572° F (300° C). Meanwhile, Walther Nernst [German: 1864–1941] synthesized small amounts of ammonia from gases at very high pressures. Combining Nernst's technique with his own,

Hall, Charles Martin

Chemist: invented inexpensive way to make aluminum
Born: December 6, 1863, Thompson, Ohio
Died: December 27, 1914, Daytona, Florida

 Aluminum is abundant in Earth's crust but before 1886 removing this lightweight, nonrusting metal from its ore was difficult and expensive. As a result, aluminum cost as much as silver and had limited use.

Hall became interested in producing aluminum inexpensively in 1880, as a freshman at Oberlin College.

Aluminum hubcap

He performed experiments in laboratories both at home and at Oberlin, and in 1886 discovered the electrolytic process of making aluminum. In this process, aluminum oxide is dissolved in a bath of molten cryolite, a rare mineral from Greenland. When electric current is passed through the mixture, the aluminum oxide separates into aluminum and oxygen. The aluminum is heavier than the cryolite and sinks to the bottom of the container.

The process was invented simultaneously by another young man of the same age, Paul Héroult [French: 1863–1914]. Now known as the Hall-Héroult process, it led to the age of aluminum, with the metal inexpensive and available enough to be used in aircraft, automobiles, packaging, and many other products.

See also electrolysis.

🖥📖 RESOURCES

• MORE ABOUT CHARLES MARTIN HALL.

http://www.acs.org/landmarks/electrochem/
http://www.invent.org/book/book-text/51.html
http://www.oberlin.edu/chem/history/cmh/cmharticle.html

Haller, Albrecht von

Biologist: founder of experimental physiology
Born: October 16, 1708, Bern, Switzerland
Died: December 12, 1777, Bern, Switzerland

 Haller changed the study of **anatomy** from an observational science to an experimental science and laid the foundation for the modern study of **physiology**. In 1672, **Francis Glisson** proposed that living tissue has a property called "irritability"—that is, an ability to contract when stimulated. On the basis of hundreds

Albrecht von Haller

of experiments, Haller proved that only muscle tissue has this property. He showed that a stimulus applied directly to a muscle causes the muscle to contract. He also showed that a stimulus applied to a nerve does not change the nerve but causes the muscle connected to the nerve to contract.

FAMOUS FIRST

In 1747, Haller published the first textbook of physiology.

Haller gave the first correct description of the mechanism of respiration, showing that the two lungs do not contract independently, as had been proposed. He showed that heart function is involuntary and automatic, and discovered that bile helps digest fats.

 **RESOURCES**

• ALBRECHT VON HALLER (1708–1777)
**http://hsc.virginia.edu/hs-library/
historical/classics/Haller.html**

Halley, Edmond

Astronomer: discovered comets travel in orbits
Born: November 8, 1656, London, England
Died: January 14, 1742, Greenwich, England

 As the 18th century began, people believed that each comet they observed was on a one-way trip, streaking through the solar system never to be seen again. Based on his own computations, historical records, and **Isaac Newton**'s ideas about gravitation, Halley in 1705 wrote that comets travel in orbits that periodically bring them back to Earth's vicinity. He believed that the comet he had seen in 1682 was the same one that people had seen in 1456, 1531, and 1607.

Edmond Halley

He predicted that this comet would return again in 1758. On Christmas night 1758, 16 years after Halley's death, an amateur astronomer in Germany became the first

Comet Halley

person to witness the return of what today is called Comet Halley.

Halley's contributions to science began in 1676, when he traveled to Saint Helena, an island in the southern Atlantic Ocean, to catalogue the unmapped stars of the Southern Hemisphere. He determined the celestial longitude and latitude of approximately 350 stars and observed a transit of Mercury across the Sun, noting that such transits can be used to determine the distance from Earth to the Sun.

In 1710, after comparing the current positions of stars with positions listed in **Claudius Ptolemy**'s star catalog, Halley correctly concluded that stars have motions of their own. This contradicted the belief, held since ancient times, that stars have fixed positions.

Halley also studied weather, explaining the cause of monsoon winds and the relation between weather and barometric pressure.

John Harrison

 RESOURCES

- Cook, Alan H. *Edmond Halley: Charting the Heavens and the Seas*. New York: Clarendon, 1998.
- EDMOND HALLEY.
  http://es.rice.edu/ED/humsoc/Galileo/Catalog/Files/halley.html

Harrison, John

Watchmaker: built the first chronometer
Born: March 1693, Foulky, England
Died: March 24, 1776, London, England

 After a series of naval disasters caused by poor navigation, the British Parliament in 1714 offered a large monetary prize for a practical way to establish a ship's longitude with a high degree of accuracy. Latitude, the north-south position, is easily determined from the stars or Sun. One known way to find longitude, or east-west position, requires knowing the exact time both at a fixed location and at the ship's position. But in 1714 all clocks lost or gained seconds or minutes daily.

Harrison began as a carpenter and in 1713 constructed his first clock completely from wood. In the 1720s, he developed more accurate clocks than previously available, achieving accuracy to within 1 second a month.

In 1728, Harrison designed a clock intended to win the longitude prize. In 1736 the clock was tested at sea. It succeeded better than the ship's regular method of navigation, but was too large and delicate for shipboard. With government backing, Harrison built two more clocks, but did not test them at sea for various reasons. The fourth clock, finished in 1759, was a totally different design. It passed all sea tests, and Harrison was awarded half the prize in 1765—the other half was withheld in part because some of the judges still hoped to win part of the prize for themselves. In 1772 King George III tested one of Harrison's clocks, which are called chronometers, and forced the government to give Harrison the remainder of his prize money.

Imitations of Harrison's chronometers were the mainstay of naval navigation throughout the 19th century and well into the 20th, when radio, loran, and global positioning replaced them.

 RESOURCES

- Sobel, Dava. *The Illustrated Longitude.* New York: Walker, 1998.
- MORE ABOUT JOHN HARRISON.
  http://www.rog.nmm.ac.uk/museum/harrison/

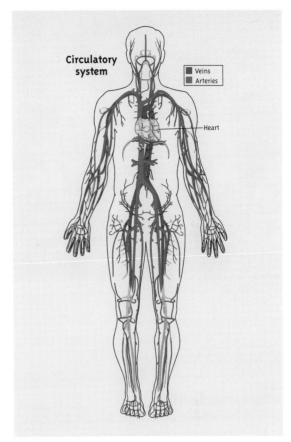

The human circulatory system

Harvey, William

Anatomist: discovered blood circulation
Born: April 1, 1578, Folkestone, England
Died: June 3, 1657, Roehampton, England

 Before Harvey, many theories about the circulation of blood had been proposed, all of them incorrect. As a young man, Harvey traveled to Padua, Italy, to study with the most famous physician and **anatomy** teacher of the time, **Hieronymus Fabricius**. Fabricius' interest in blood vessels greatly influenced Harvey's research.

Harvey carefully studied the structure of the heart and blood vessels in many animals, including snails, insects, fish, frogs, birds, and mammals. He observed the movement of blood and watched what happened when he interfered with blood flow in arteries and veins. In 1628, Harvey published *Anatomical Study on the Movement of the Heart and Blood in Animals*. This book accurately explained that blood flows in a circular path: the heart pumps blood into arteries, which carry the blood throughout the body, and the blood returns to the heart through veins. Harvey also showed that valves in the veins, discovered by Fabricius, prevent blood from flowing backward. Harvey's theory was extremely controversial because it contradicted long-held beliefs and because he could not explain how blood passes from arteries

William Harvey

to veins—a discovery that awaited the invention of microscopes and their use by **Marcello Malpighi.**

 RESOURCES

- Avraham, Regina. *Circulatory System*. Broomall, PA: Chelsea House, 1999. (JUV/YA)
- Yount, Lisa. *William Harvey: Discoverer of How Blood Circulates*. Berkeley Heights, NJ: Enslow, 1994. (JUV/YA)
- DISCOVERY OF THE CIRCULATION OF THE BLOOD.

  http://www.usyd.edu.au/su/hps/tutes/ lecture18.html
- WILLIAM HARVEY.

  http://www2.cwrl.utexas.edu/scoggins/ britishprojects/seventeenth/Harvey.html

Hawking, Stephen

Physicist: explained properties of black holes
Born: January 8, 1942, Oxford, England

 "Black holes ain't so black," says Hawking. Hawking became interested in black holes—collapsed **stars** with so much mass that scientists believed that nothing, not even light, could escape their

gravitational force—early in his career. In 1974, he calculated that under certain conditions black holes leak radiation that forms initially as "virtual" **subatomic particles**—particles that appear and usually disappear in an instant, but that can persist near black holes. The particles came to be called Hawking radiation. They were the first indication of the intimate relationship that exists among gravity, subatomic particles, and heat.

The major goal of Hawking's career has been to discover the theory of everything. Such a "unified theory," which other scientists also are pursuing, would link all 4 of the basic forces in the universe—gravity,

Stephen Hawking

electromagnetism, and strong and weak nuclear forces. A unified theory would explain how the **universe** was created and how it works.

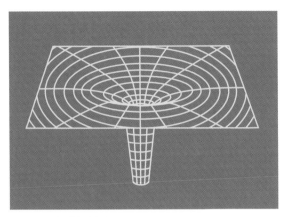

Diagram of a black hole

Hawking is a noted author and lecturer. Because he suffers from amyotrophic lateral sclerosis (Lou Gehrig's disease), he is confined to a wheelchair and communicates via a computer and voice synthesizer.

 RESOURCES

- Filkin, David. *Stephen Hawking's Universe: The Cosmos Explained.* New York: Basic, 1998.
- McDaniel, Melissa. *Stephen Hawking: Revolutionary Physicist.* Broomall, PA: Chelsea House, 1994. (JUV/YA)
- STEPHEN W. HAWKING'S WEB PAGE.

  http://www.hawking.org.uk

Hearing Aids

Horns ➤ Development of microphone ➤ Development of electric hearing aid ➤ **DE FOREST** (amplifier) ➤ **House** (cochlear implant) ➤ Development of aids with batteries ➤ Development of digital sound

 Hearing loss ranges from slight difficulty in hearing soft or high-pitched tones to total inability to

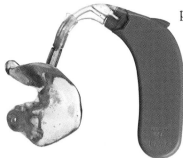

A hearing aid

perceive sound.

Failure or impairment can occur at any age, but about 1 in 4 persons aged 65 to 75 experiences some hearing loss and nearly half over 75 do.

Hearing occurs when sound waves produce a response that is transmitted to the brain. The simplest form of hearing aid increases volume. Horns with a large opening that taper to a small earpiece collect sound waves and slightly compress them, increasing volume. Before the 1900s, horns were the only form of hearing aid. In 1878, the first microphone was invented and by 1902 an electric hearing aid existed. **Lee De Forest's** 1907 amplifier was the next advance. Volume-increasing hearing aids since combine a microphone and amplifier.

People want hearing aids to be small and inconspicuous. In 1952, hearing aids became the first application of transistors and in 1964 the first devices to use integrated circuits. One model in the 1950s was built into eyeglasses and, by the 1970s, aids complete with batteries could be contained in the outer ear. Lithium batteries, invented in 1985, are longer-lasting and smaller—some aids now fit inside the ear canal. Improvements from the 1990s include digital sound and aids that increase soft sounds more than loud ones or amplify specific frequencies.

The cochlear implant attacks hearing problems in a different way. First developed by William F. House [American: 1923–] in 1961, implants turn sounds into electrical impulses that directly stimulate auditory nerve cells. Sounds produced by cochlear implants are not exactly the same as those created by mechanisms in the ear, however.

RESOURCES

• MORE ABOUT HEARING AIDS.

http://www.betterhearing.org/hearaido.htm

http://www.pbs.org/wnet/soundandfury/cochlear/hearingaids.html

Heat

ARISTOTLE (theory of heat as quality) ➤ **Empedocles** (theory of heat as a substance) ➤ **Democritus** (heat as motion of atoms) ➤ **THOMPSON** (heat produced by motion) ➤ **MAXWELL**/Boltzmann (thermodynamics)

Since ancient times three theories of heat have competed for acceptance. **Aristotle** considered heat, which can be felt, a quality, like color or length. Empedocles [Greek: c. 492– c. 432 B.C.E.] thought heat was a substance, like air or water. Democritus [Greek: c. 470– c. 320 B.C.E.] and followers, howev-

The sun is a source of radiant heat.

er, proposed that heat is the motion of atoms. Most people accepted Aristotle's view until the Scientific Revolution of the 1600s.

Temperature is different from heat

The idea that heat is a substance, named caloric, became the leading theory of the 1700s. An experiment by **Benjamin Thompson**, Count Rumford, in 1798, however, showed great amounts of heat produced by motion. Thereafter, the concept that heat is the motion of particles was generally accepted. In the 1800s, heat was recognized as a form of energy, necessary for **conservation laws** to work. Important mathematical studies from 1859 through 1877 by **James Clerk Maxwell** and Ludwig Boltzmann [Austrian: 1844–1906] established how particles interact with each other in gases to produce the laws of heat, called thermodynamics.

Scientists of the 1900s recognized that heat can be measured only when particle motion is transferred from 1 substance to another. Thus, heat today is defined as transfer of energy resulting from temperature differences. Heat can be measured in calories—one calorie is the amount of heat needed to raise a gram of water 1°C, but since heat is a form of energy, scientists use the energy measure, the joule (1 calorie is about 4.184 joules). Note that temperature is not the same as heat.

RESOURCES

- Gardner, Robert, and Eric Kerner. *Science Projects about Temperature and Heat.* Berkeley Heights, NJ: Enslow, 1994. (JUV/YA)
- Goldstein, Martin. *The Refrigerator and the Universe: Understanding the Laws of Energy.* Cambridge, MA: Harvard University, 1993.
- MORE ABOUT HEAT.

  http://www.unidata.ucar.edu/staff/blynds/tmp.html - Heat

Helicopters

China (toy tops) ➤ **CAYLEY** (flying top) ➤ **Cornu** (first to rise above the ground with passengers) ➤ **France** (steered) ➤ **Cierva** (autogiro) ➤ **SIKORSKY** (modern helicopter)

A helicopter is a flying machine using lift supplied by powered propellers called rotors. Chinese toy tops from as early as the 4th century C.E. spun rotors to rise more than 20 feet (6 m) into the air. In 1825, **George Cayley** built an improved top that rose some 90 feet (30 m).

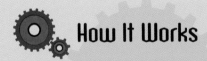

How It Works

The helicopter rotor pushes air downward, giving upward lift. Special hinges attach the blade to the shaft. These adjust the angle of each blade separately, allowing for changing direction of flight and amount of lift.

In the 20th century, people built helicopters that could lift humans and cargo. Bicycle mechanic Paul Cornu [French: 1881–1944] developed the first to rise off the ground in 1907. By 1924, various

A modern helicopter

improvements led to a French helicopter that could be steered, although it was too unstable for practical use. At that time Juan de Cierva [Spanish: 1895-1936] invented the autogiro. Autogiros combine a propeller for forward motion with a large unpowered rotor for lift. As the propeller pulls the craft forward, air flows past the rotor, which begins to spin and provides the lift.

Other inventors seized concepts behind the autogiro's rotor to make helicopters that could take off and land vertically and also be steered in level flight. In 1936, the German military tested such a helicopter, while the U.S. Army funded **Igor I. Sikorsky's** flight research. A Sikorsky helicopter in 1942

flew 761 miles (1,225 km) from Ohio to Connecticut.

A few helicopters saw action on both sides during World War II. After the war, many expected helicopters to replace the automobile. Instead, they became versatile military aircraft with limited civilian use.

RESOURCES

- Hawkes, Nigel. *Planes and Other Aircraft* (How Machines Work). Brookfield, CT: Copper Beech, 1999. (JUV/YA)
- HELICOPTER HISTORY.
  http://www.helis.com/
  http://www.ai.mit.edu/projects/cbcl/heli/helo_history.html

Helmholtz, Hermann von

Physiologist, physicist: invented an ophthalmoscope
Born: August 31, 1821, Potsdam, Germany
Died: September 8, 1894, Berlin, Germany

  In 1851, Helmholtz invented an ophthalmoscope, which allows doctors to examine the inside of the eye. It has a light source for illumination and a mirror with a hole in the center through which the doctor looks at the eye; lenses can be rotated into the hole to make images clearer. (**Charles Babbage** had invented an ophthalmoscope in 1847 but his version did not become known.)

Helmholtz proved that the eye's ability to focus at different distances depends on automatic changes in the convexity of the lens. He also helped pioneer the study of color. He commented in 1857 that "the eye cannot separate combined colors from each other; it sees them as an unresolvable, simple sensation of one

Hermann von Helmholtz

mixed color." He extended a theory proposed by **Thomas Young**, demonstrating that any hue perceived by the eye is a mix of only three colors of light: red, blue, and green.

Helmholtz also made important contributions in the fields of acoustics, nerve reflexes, electric currents, and the law of conservation of energy.

 RESOURCES

- COLOR PHYSICS.
  http://keystone.geog.ucsb.edu/geog115a/ Reference/younghemltheory.html

- IMPORTANT DATES IN VISION SCIENCE.
  http://aris.ss.uci.edu/cogsci/vision/ yellott_dates.html

Helmont, Jan Baptista van

Chemist, physician: showed plants need water for growth
Born: January 1579, Brussels, Belgium
Died: December 30, 1644, near Vilvorde, Belgium

  Helmont is best remembered for an experiment that "proved" an incorrect idea. Before people knew about **photosynthesis**, Helmont put 200 pounds (91 kg) of dry soil in a large pot, moistened it with water, and planted in it a willow stem weighing 5 pounds (2.3 kg). For the next 5 years he added only water to the pot. Then he separated the tree from the soil. The tree had gained about 164 pounds (74 kg) while the soil weight had decreased by only 3 ounces (85 g). Since the only thing added to the pot was water, Helmont concluded that plants "proceed out of the Element of water only."

Helmont did not suspect that gases play a role in plant growth. Yet he was the first scientist to realize that there are gases distinct from atmospheric air. He recognized that the gas given off by burning charcoal is the same as that produced by fermenting grapes—now known to be carbon dioxide. He even invented the term "*gas!*"

 **RESOURCES**

• VAN HELMONT'S EXPERIMENT.
http://www.nsta.org/Energy/find/primer/primer2_3.html

Henry, Joseph

Physicist: studied electromagnetism
Born: December 17, 1797, Albany, New York
Died: May 13, 1878, Washington, D.C.

 In the 1820s Henry began building electromagnets, improving on the design of William Sturgeon [English: 1783– 1850] by wrapping many turns of wire around a horseshoe-shaped bar. One of his electromagnets was powerful enough to lift a ton.

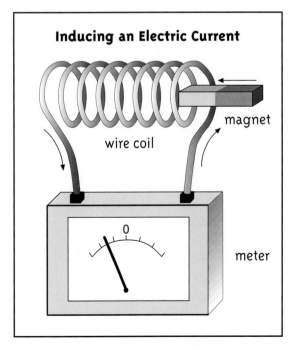

Inducing an Electric Current

wire coil

magnet

meter

0

Henry then discovered that current flowing through a wire generates a magnetic field that causes electric current to flow through a second wire. Based on this, Henry placed two wires close together; when electric current began to flow through one wire a spurt of current was induced in the second wire. Unfortunately, Henry was slow to publish these discoveries; as a result, **Michael Faraday** is generally credited with the discovery of electromagnetic induction. But the unit of measure of the magnetic fields produced by a current is called the henry.

FAMOUS FIRST

In 1846, Henry became the first director of the newly founded Smithsonian Institution in Washington, D.C.—the oldest professional scientific research organization in the United States.

Henry built the first electric motor and invented the electric relay that made possible the long-distance **telegraph** of **Samuel F. B. Morse**. He made the first step-down electric transformer, in which electric current is increased but voltage is decreased.

Later in his career Henry was the first to measure the temperature of the Sun. He found that sunspots are cooler than the Sun's surrounding surface.

 **RESOURCES**

• A HOLE IN THE FLOOR.
http://www.150.si.edu/chap2/two.htm

Hero of Alexandria

Mechanic and mathematician: invented early
  mechanical devices
Lived: c. 60, Alexandria, Egypt

 Hero's fascination with mechanics led
him to invent dozens of devices operated by water, steam, or compressed
air. These included an organ driven by water
power, fountains, siphons, and steam-powered
machines. He also invented coin-operated
machines and all sorts of engines. Many of
his devices were meant to amuse or mystify
and had no practical purpose.

FAMOUS FIRST

Hero's inventions included the aeolipile,
sometimes called the first **steam engine**.
It had a sphere mounted on a boiler and
two nozzles. Escaping steam caused the
sphere to rotate. Ferdinand Verbiest
[Flemish: 1623–1688] built a version of the
engine in the 1670s, using it to move a
cart a few inches.

Hero wrote a number of books, some
of which survive to this day. *Pneumatica*
describes many of his inventions; *Dioptra* is
a book on land surveying; *Catoptrica* covers
light, including the law of reflection; and
Mechanica discusses simple machines and
mechanical problems of daily life. His most
important mathematical work was *Metrica*,
in which he presented formulas for finding
the area of triangles, circles, polygons, and
other geometric figures.

 RESOURCES

• THE PNEUMATICS OF HERO OF ALEXANDRIA.
  http://www.history.rochester.edu/steam/
  hero/index.html

Herschel, William

Astronomer: discovered Uranus
Born: November 15, 1738, Hanover, Germany
Died: August 25, 1822, Slough, England

 Like many early astronomers,
Herschel built his own telescopes,
grinding mirrors and making the
large tubes and mountings needed to
house them. His most important discovery
occurred in 1781 when he examined small

FAMOUS FIRST

The first invisible electromagnetic radiation to be discovered was infrared radiation, found by Herschel in 1800 while
studying sunlight.

stars in the constellation Gemini. One of
the stars caught his attention because of
its size. He observed it for several months
before announcing that it wasn't a star but

William Herschel

a planet. Beyond Saturn in our solar system, it was named Uranus. Six years later he discovered and named Titania and Oberon, 2 moons of Uranus. He also discovered 2 of Saturn's moons.

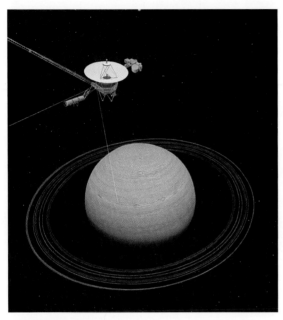

Uranus, discovered by Herschel in 1781, was visited by the space probe Voyager 2 in 1986.

Herschel tried to map our **galaxy**, the Milky Way—"this magnificent collection of stars," he called it. But thousands of bright patches called nebulas obstructed his view. He correctly guessed that many nebulas are immense clouds of gas while others are galaxies of stars outside the Milky Way—a theory not proven until the 20th century.

 RESOURCES

- MORE ABOUT WILLIAM HERSCHEL.
  http://www.bath-preservation-trust.org.uk/ herschel/
  http://astronomica.org/Gallery/ dead_astronomer/dead_astronomer20.html

Hertz, Heinrich

Physicist: produced and observed radio waves
Born: February 22, 1857, Hamburg, Germany
Died: January 1, 1894, Bonn, Germany

 Hertz in the 1880s worked on experimental confirmation of **James Clerk Maxwell's** 1873 theory of electromagnetism. In the process, Hertz recognized that according to Maxwell's equations a moving electric charge should produce detectable waves. In 1887 he built a device that made an electric spark move rapidly back and forth (oscillate) across a small gap between 2 metal conductors. In 1888 he used a loop of wire with a similar gap as a detector. When the spark oscillated, a weak spark also appeared in the detector. With this simple apparatus, Hertz determined the charge's wavelength and showed that the waves behave like light waves, except for being much longer. He had discovered what we now call radio waves.

YEARBOOK: 1887

- Hertz discovers the photoelectric effect.
- Gottlieb Daimler builds the first automobile.
- The first contact lens is invented.
- The Michelson-Morley experiment shows light is unaffected by Earth's motion.

Hertz made a second discovery in 1887 with his sending apparatus. The spark travels farther when ultraviolet light shines on the metal. Hertz reported this, later called the photoelectric effect, but did not pursue it. To explain the photoelectric effect, **Albert Einstein** concluded in 1905 that electromagnetic waves also behave as particles called photons.

See also photoelectric phenomena.

 **RESOURCES**

• Buchwald, Jed Z. *The Creation of Scientific Effects: Heinrich Hertz and Electric Waves.* Chicago: University of Chicago, 1994.

Hipparchus

Astronomer and mathematician: first to apply mathematics to astronomy
Born: about 190 B.C.E., Nicaea, Macedonian Empire (now Iznik, Turkey)
Died: about 120 B.C.E., possibly at Rhodes

 Little is known of Hipparchus' life and most of his original works are lost. Early in his career, Hipparchus invented trigonometry, the branch of mathematics that includes indirect measurement of distances.

Hipparchus calculated the distance from Earth to the Moon.

FAMOUS FIRST

Using trigonometry, Hipparchus made the first star map, locating about 850 stars and listing them by magnitude, a numerical measurement of brightness that he invented.

Many consider Hipparchus the greatest astronomer of antiquity. He correctly calculated the distance from Earth to the Moon. He recognized that Earth's axis wobbles very slightly, returning to its original position every 26,000 years. This wobble is called precession, and he used this in his calculation of the length of a year to within 6.5 minutes. Finally, he originated the idea that motions of the Moon and planets could be explained in terms of small circles, called epicycles, riding on otherwise circular orbits. This mathematical theory, refined by **Claudius Ptolemy**, successfully predicted apparent movements of planets but was replaced by the discovery that planets orbit the Sun in elliptical paths.

 **RESOURCES**

• MORE ABOUT HIPPARCHUS.

http://www-groups.dcs.st-and.ac.uk/history/Mathematicians/Hipparchus.html

Hippocrates

Physician: "Father of Medicine"
Born: c. 460 B.C.E., Cos, Greece
Died: c. 377 B.C.E., near Larissa, Greece

 To this day, newly graduated physicians take an oath as they begin their medical practice. Known as the Hippocratic Oath, it embodies a code of ethics detailing the rights of patients and responsibilities of physicians. The oath may have been written long after the time

Hippocrates

He was the first physician who stressed the importance of studying the body as a whole rather than as a collection of separate parts. He also was the first to believe that ideas and feelings come from the brain rather than the heart.

Hippocrates mistakenly believed that living matter is made up of 4 "humors"—blood, yellow bile, black bile, and phlegm—with good health depending on the humors being mixed in the right proportion. This theory greatly influenced physicians for more than 2,000 years before being disproved in the 1700s.

 RESOURCES

- Byers, James M. *From Hippocrates to Virchow: Reflections on Human Disease.* Chicago: ASCP, 1987.
- OATH OF HIPPOCRATES.
  http://www.softcode.com/oath_hip.html
- WRITINGS OF HIPPOCRATES.
  http://www.vt.edu/vt98/academics/books/hippocrates/HippocratesIndex.html

of Hippocrates. Nonetheless, it is appropriately named, for Hippocrates moved medicine away from superstition, making it a scientific undertaking, and established moral and professional standards for physicians.

At the time of Hippocrates, **disease** was thought to be inflicted by gods or other supernatural beings. But Hippocrates believed that illness has a physical explanation. He listened to his patients, made careful records of his observations, and took a rational approach to healing. For instance, he believed that rest, fresh air, a good diet, and cleanliness help the healing process.

Hodgkin, Dorothy Crowfoot

Chemist: a founder of protein crystallography
Born: May 12, 1910, Cairo, Egypt
Died: July 29, 1994, Shipston-on-Stour, England

 Crystallography—the study of the structure of crystals—was born early in the 20th century, when several scientists discovered that the atoms in a crystal diffract X rays, creating a pattern that can be captured on film. Using mathematical calculations on this pattern, it then is possible to determine the three-dimensional arrangement of atoms in the crystal. However, this method was difficult and time-consuming to apply, especially for complex molecules such as those produced by living organisms. Biochemists paid little attention to the technology.

NOBEL PRIZE 1964

Hodgkin was awarded the Nobel Prize in chemistry "for her determination by X-ray techniques of the structures of biologically important molecules."

Then along came Hodgkin, who had been fascinated by crystals since childhood. In 1934, when a co-worker made the first X-ray diffraction photograph of a protein crystal, pepsin, Hodgkin analyzed the data to determine pepsin's structure and molecular weight. She went on to develop improved techniques and used X-ray crystallography to determine the structure of cholesterol, penicillin, vitamin B_{12}, and dozens of additional proteins, all far more complex than anything studied previously. She showed, for example, that the insulin molecule consists of 777 atoms.

 **RESOURCES**

• MORE ABOUT DOROTHY CROWFOOT HODGKIN.

http://www.nobel.se/chemistry/laureates/1964/hodgkin-bio.html

http://curie.che.virginia.edu/scientist/hodgkin.html

Hollerith, Herman

Engineer: used punched cards to process data
Born: February 29, 1860, Buffalo, New York
Died: November 17, 1929, Washington, D.C.

 Every 10 years the U.S. government conducts a census of the nation's population. In 1880 it took a few

Herman Hollerith

months to do the headcount—and years to tabulate and analyze the data, with everything done by hand. Clearly, a new system had to be found before the 1890 census.

Hollerith began working on the problem in 1882. He built a tabulating machine that used rolls of perforated paper tape, much like the tape developed by **Joseph-Marie Jacquard** for his loom system. The position of each hole punched on the tape indicated a bit of information, such as a person's age or occupation. As the tape moved past metal brushes in the machine, any brush passing over a hole closed an electric circuit, thereby advancing a counter. But the system had flaws. For example, finding a particular bit of information meant searching the entire tape.

The solution came as Hollerith watched a train conductor punch characteristics of passengers on paper tickets. This led Hollerith to build a machine that used individual punched cards instead of tape. The cards could be easily corrected, replaced, or sorted in useful ways—for example, sifting out and analyzing all cards representing farmers.

Hollerith's machine was used for the 1890 census, saving much time and money. In 1897, Hollerith established the Tabulating Machine Company, which merged in 1911 with two other companies and eventually became IBM, one of the giants in the **computer** industry. Hollerith's concept of punched cards was used in computers until the late 1960s.

 **RESOURCES**

• MORE ABOUT HERMAN HOLLERITH.

http://www.invent.org/book/book-text/57.html

http://www.lis.pitt.edu/mbsclass/is2000/hall_of_fame/hollerit.htm

Hooke, Robert

Physicist, inventor: discovered cells
Born: July 18, 1635, Freshwater, England
Died: March 3, 1703, London, England

  Hooke carried out investigations in many fields and designed numerous scientific instruments. His best-known discovery, reported in 1665, occurred as he looked at thin slices of cork through a compound microscope he had built. He saw that cork consists of tiny units, and he named these units "cells." He also was the first person known to have examined **fossils** through a microscope, noting similarities and differences between shells of fossil and living mollusks.

A study of elasticity led to formulation of what is now called Hooke's Law. This states that an elastic object stretches or bends in direct proportion to the amount of force acting on the object. Using an air pump he designed while working with **Robert Boyle**, Hooke demonstrated the importance of air to the processes of

Cells were first seen and named by Robert Hooke.

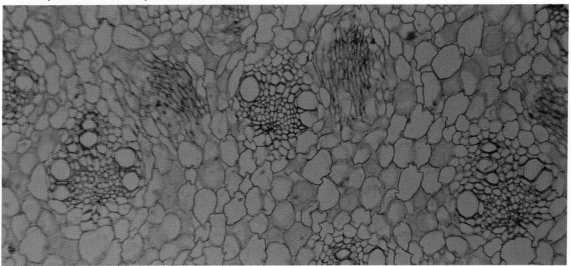

burning and breathing. He analyzed flames, noting that the interior of a flame does not emit light.

Hooke built and designed his own telescope, with which he observed craters on the Moon, the rotation of Mars, and a double star. He discovered that Jupiter revolves on its axis and carried out the first detailed investigation of a comet's nucleus and tail.

Hooke's inventions included the anemometer, an instrument for measuring wind speed; the balance spring used in watches; and the universal joint that allows rotation to be transmitted from one shaft to another.

 RESOURCES

- Drake, Ellen T. *Restless Genius: Robert Hooke and His Earthly Thoughts*. New York: Oxford University, 1996.
- MORE ABOUT ROBERT HOOKE.

  http://www.rod/beavon.clara.net/leonardo.htm

  http://www.ucmp.berkeley.edu/history/hooke.html

Hopper, Grace Murray

Mathematician: early computer programmer
Born: December 9, 1906, New York, New York
Died: January 1, 1992, Arlington, Virginia

  Computers use a machine language consisting of only two digits, 0 and 1. Programmers of early computers had to work in this language or in simple codes that could be assembled into machine language. This was laborious and easily subject to error. A much more practical method would be employing languages that use ordinary words and phrases—

Grace Hopper

so-called high-level languages. In 1951, Hopper wrote the first compiler, a program that translates instructions written in high-level language into machine language.

FAMOUS FIRST

One day in the 1940s, when Hopper was working on the Mark I computer at Harvard University, the computer failed. Hopper and her colleagues discovered that a moth had short-circuited a connection. The moth was removed and placed in a logbook with the note, "first actual bug found." Today, the term "bug" is commonly used to describe any error in computer hardware or software that prevents it from running correctly.

Other researchers adapted Hopper's techniques, developing new compilers and high-level languages for mathematical and scientific applications. Hopper began working on a program for business-oriented tasks, such as payroll calculation. Named Flow-matic, it greatly influenced development of COBOL (COmmon Business-Oriented Language), a widely used business language that first appeared in 1959. Hopper led efforts to standardize COBOL so it could be used on different computer models.

RESOURCES

- Whitelaw, Nancy. *Grace Hopper, Programming Pioneer.* New York: W.H. Freeman, 1995.
- MORE ABOUT GRACE MURRAY HOPPER.

  http://www.cs.yale.edu/tap/Files/hopper-story.html

  http://www.norfolk.navy.mil/chips/grace_hopper/womn.htm

Hormones

 ADDISON (founded modern endocrinology; adrenal glands) ➤ **Berthold** (testes) ➤ **Starling/Bayliss** (secretin/"hormone") ➤ **Cushing** (hormones interlinked) ➤ **BANTING** (insulin)

Hormones are potent chemicals secreted into the blood by endocrine glands. They regulate certain body activities; for example, thyroxin made in the thyroid regulates the rate of **metabolism**.

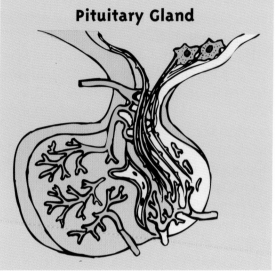

Pituitary Gland

The pituitary gland produces a number of hormones.

Modern endocrinology—the study of endocrine glands and their hormones—began with the work of **Thomas Addison**, who in 1849 reported that the adrenal glands are necessary for life. That same year Arnold A. Berthold [German: 1803–1861] demonstrated that the testes have another function besides producing sperm, and suggested that they secreted a substance that is carried by the blood. However, Berthold's paper was ignored for more than 60 years.

FAMOUS FIRST

Plants also produce chemical messengers, known as auxins, gibberellins, and cytokinins. Fritz Went [Dutch: 1863–1935], a graduate student in Holland, isolated the first such compound in 1926.

Proof that the blood carries substances from organs where they are produced to organs they influence came from Ernest

Starling [English: 1866–1927] and William Bayliss [English: 1860–1924]. In 1902, they discovered that as food moves from the stomach into the small intestine, cells in the wall of the small intestine produce a substance they called secretin. They went on to prove that secretin is carried by the blood to the pancreas, stimulating it to release a digestive juice. Starling gave the name "hormone" to secretin and similar substances. By 1912, Harvey Cushing [American: 1869–1939] showed that hormones are interlinked, with hormones from the pituitary gland controlling other endocrine glands.

YEARBOOK: 1905

- Starling introduces the word "hormone."
- **Albert Einstein** publishes his theory of special relativity.
- Percival Lowell [American: 1855–1916] predicts the existence of a **planet** beyond Neptune.
- Clarence McClung [American: 1870–1946] discovers that female mammals have two X **chromosomes** and males have one X and one Y.

Isolation of hormones aided efforts to identify the roles played by these substances in **diseases** and led to improved methods of treating illness. Therapeutic use of hormones began in 1921, when **Frederick Banting** and colleagues administered insulin, a hormone produced by certain cells of the pancreas, to a person with diabetes.

Initially, hormones were laboriously extracted from animal tissues. Development of **genetic engineering** technologies in the last decades of the 20th century led to efficient production of pure human hormones.

RESOURCES

- MORE ABOUT HORMONES.

  http://www.ohsuhealth.com/endocrine/index.asp

  http://nobel.sdsc.edu/chemistry/laureates/1955/press.html

  http://www.plant-hormones.bbsrc.ac.uk/education/Kenh.htm#discovered

Hovercraft

As early as 1716, inventors began to try to employ a cushion of air to reduce drag as a boat moves through water. These early designs failed because lightweight engines that could produce sufficient air

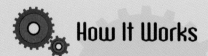 **How It Works**

Unlike a rocket, which moves in response to mass expelled from the engine, a hovercraft's propeller compresses air between the craft and the surface immediately below, providing lift before air escapes at edges. This lift is called the ground effect; another name for hovercraft is ground-effect machine.

pressure were not available until the 20th century. In 1950, Christopher Cockerell [English: 1910–1999] also tried to use air as a lubricant for boats, but soon realized that to travel over waves, the air cushion had to lift the entire craft above the water. By 1955, he had built a model that accomplished

A hovercraft

this using compressed air, which he called a hovercraft. In 1959, the first full-size craft was built, demonstrating its abilities by crossing the English Channel. Improved versions began passenger service along the coast of Great Britain in 1962.

RESOURCES
- HOVERCRAFT HISTORY AND MUSEUM SITE.
  http://www.hover.globalinternet.co.uk/

Hubble, Edwin

Astronomer: showed universe is expanding
Born: November 20, 1889, Marshfield, Missouri
Died: September 28, 1953, San Marino, California

In 1924, Hubble confirmed the existence of **galaxies** outside our own galaxy, the Milky Way. He accom-

plished this by calculating the distances to the Cepheids, stars that vary in brightness in predictable ways. He found, for example, that a Cepheid in the Andromeda galaxy was about 1 million light years away. Since the Milky Way's diameter is 100,000 light years or less, Andromeda clearly lies outside it. Hubble went on to measure the distances to 9 galaxies. Then in 1925 he developed a system for classifying galaxies based on their shapes, which is still used today.

Notable Quotable

Equipped with his five senses, man explores the universe around him and calls the adventure Science.

—Edwin Hubble

Hubble Space Telescope

Another astronomer, Vesto Slipher [American: 1875–1969], noticed that some galaxies were moving rapidly away from the Milky Way. Hubble focused on the speed of galaxies and in 1929 provided

How It Works

Hubble's discovery about the speed of various galaxies made use of the Doppler effect, enunciated by Christian Doppler [Austrian: 1803–1853] in 1842. This principle says that if a source of light or sound waves moves in relation to an observer, the observer detects frequency changes in the waves. For instance, as a galaxy moves away from Earth, light waves that reach our instruments decrease in frequency, toward the red end of the spectrum. The greater the galaxy's speed, the greater this "redshift."

the first evidence that the **universe** isn't unchanging, as had been widely assumed, but is expanding. He developed what is now called Hubble's law, which says that the further away a galaxy is from Earth, the faster it is moving away from us.

 RESOURCES

• Christianson, Gale E. *Edwin Hubble: Mariner of the Nebulae*. Chicago: University of Chicago, 1996.

• MORE ABOUT EDWIN HUBBLE.

http://www.pbs.org/wgbh/aso/databank/entries/bahubb.html

http://antwrp.gsfc.nasa.gov/diamond_jubilee/d_1996/sandage_hubble.html

http://www.hubbleconstant.com/

Human Genome Project

Sanger/Gilbert (techniques to read DNA) ➤ First genome (virus) mapping ➤ First bacterium mapped ➤ First plant genome mapped ➤ **WATSON** (heads human project) ➤ First interpretations of human genome published

 One of the major scientific projects underway as the 21st century began was the effort to map the human genome—that is, the entire sequence of units that makes up human **DNA**, including our **genes**. Knowing the complete genome and then exploring the role of each gene is expected to have an enormous impact on understanding human heredity and physiology. The knowledge also will be an invaluable resource for developing improved methods of treating disease using **genetic engineering** and other technologies.

Sequencing DNA information became practical in 1977, when Frederick Sanger [English: 1918–] and Walter Gilbert

Human Genome Project logo

[American: 1932–] independently developed techniques to read the 4 chemical bases that make up DNA. That same year a virus became the first organism to have its entire genome sequenced. The first bacterium genome was sequenced in 1995, the first animal (the worm *Caenorhabditis elegans*) in 1998, and the first plant (the mustard *Arabidopsis thaliana*) in 2000.

In the mid-1980s, it was proposed that a large-scale effort be made to sequence the human genome. The Human Genome Project, an international, publicly financed consortium with **James D. Watson** as its first director, began in 1988. In 1998, a private venture led by **J. Craig Venter** decided to

---

Notable Quotable

It is characteristic of both science and progress that they continually open new fields to our vision.

—**Louis Pasteur**

---

compete with the government project.

In 2001, the 2 groups separately published their first interpretations of the human genome. They were in general agreement that the genome consists of a sequence of some 3.2 billion units of DNA. Within this sequence there appeared to be about 30,000 genes. Some other geneticists, however, believed that the groups missed some genes and that there may be twice as many or more.

 RESOURCES

- FROM DARWIN TO THE HUMAN GENOME PROJECT. http://www.csuchico.edu/anth/CASP/Carmosino_P.html
- LANDMARKS IN THE HISTORY OF GENETICS. http://members.tripod.com/dorakmt/genetics/notes01.html

Huygens, Christiaan

Astronomer, physicist, mathematician: recognized Saturn's rings, built pendulum clocks
Born: April 14, 1629, The Hague, Netherlands
Died: June 8, 1695, The Hague, Netherlands

  In the 1650s, using a refracting telescope he built himself, Huygens discovered the Orion nebula; Saturn's largest moon, Titan; and

---

YEARBOOK: 1659

- Huygens is the first to observe surface features of Mars.
- **Robert Hooke** helps **Robert Boyle** build an improved air pump.
- Thomas Willis [English: 1621–1675] gives first description of typhoid fever.
- The sign ÷ for division is introduced in a book by Johann Heinrich Rahn [Swiss: 1622–1676].

Notable Quotable

The world is my fatherland, science is my religion.

—Christiaan Huygens

the planetary rings of Saturn. He explained that the rings are formed at an angle to Saturn's orbit, are not solid, and have no physical connection with the planet itself. Huygens identified surface features on Mars and made the first map of the planet. Based on movement of surface features he determined the planet's size and the length of the Martian day.

Huygens also studied pendulums, making the first practical pendulum **clocks** and unsuccessfully trying to construct a workable pendulum device for determining longitude at sea.

Another area of interest was the nature of **light**. In 1678, Huygens presented his wave theory of light, saying light behaves much like an ocean wave moving through the sea. This conflicted with ideas of his contemporaries, including **Isaac Newton**, but better explained the phenomena of reflection, refraction, and diffraction. Later work by **Thomas Young** and **James Clerk Maxwell** confirmed the wave theory.

Huygens first identified the rings of Saturn

In 1690, Huygens wrote *The Discovery of Celestial Worlds: Theories about Inhabitants, Plants, and Products of Planetary Worlds.* It was the first book that speculated that the universe is populated with "so many Suns, so many Earths," and that life exists not only here but also on planets orbiting other stars.

RESOURCES

- MORE ABOUT CHRISTIAAN HUYGENS.
  http://me.in-berlin.de/jd/himmel/astro/
  Huygens-e.html
  http://www.sil.si.edu/DigitalCollections/
  HST/Huygens/huygens-introduction.htm

Ibn Sina

Physician: wrote medical encyclopedia
Born: 980, Afshana, central Asia (now Uzbekistan)
Died: 1037, Hamadan, Persia (now Iran)

Abu Ali al-Husain ibn Abdallah ibn Sina—also known by his Latinized name, Avicenna—was one of the greatest scholars of medieval times. His major contribution was the *Qanun [Canon of Medicine]*, a huge encyclopedia describing all the medical knowledge known to him. Like the work of his predecessor **Razi**, the *Qanun* became a standard medical textbook for centuries.

Another influential work written by ibn Sina was the *Al-shifa [Book of Healing]*. This was a science encyclopedia that covered plants, animals, astronomy, physics, psychology, mathematics, and many other subjects.

Although much of the knowledge in ibn Sina's works came from ancient times, some was based on his own observations. For instance, he recognized that

Ibn Sina, also known as Avicenna

tuberculosis is a contagious **disease** and that some diseases are spread through soil or water. He observed Venus as a spot against the surface of the Sun and realized this means that Venus lies between Earth and the Sun.

RESOURCES

- MEDIEVAL MEDICINE, HEALTH AND HYGIENE.
  http://www.sfusd.edu/schwww/sch618/
  islam/nbLinks/Islam_Medicine_Health.html
- ABU ALI AL-HUSAIN IBN ABDALLAH IBN SINA (AVICENNA).
  http://www-groups.dcs.st-and.ac.uk/
  history/Mathematicians/Avicenna.html

Ice Ages

Around 1800, European naturalists observed that some large rocks had moved a long distance from where they formed. Rivers of ice called glaciers had transported boulders, then dropped them when the glaciers melted. Europe, therefore, had once been much colder, since in the 1800s glaciers occurred on high mountains only. By the 1830s, some scientists began to speak of an ice age. In 1837, **Louis Agassiz** offered convincing evidence that the ice age had covered Europe with glaciers more than 10,000 years earlier.

YEARBOOK: 1837

- Agassiz proposes that Europe has experienced an ice age.
- **Samuel F.B. Morse** patents his **telegraph**.
- John Deere [U.S. 1804–1886] markets a plow sharp enough to use on prairie turf.
- Henri Dutrochet [French: 1776–1847] discovers that chlorophyll helps plants absorb carbon dioxide and emit oxygen.

Since Agassiz's day, new evidence shows there were at least 5 such ice ages, each millions of years long, when glaciers moved far beyond polar regions and mountain tops. Scientists in 1998

During ice ages, glaciers advance from polar regions and down mountainsides.

proposed that in the first 2 of these, ice advanced all the way to the equator, forming "snowball Earth." During the snowball Earth periods, most early life forms perished.

Three factors are thought to cause ice ages. **Plate tectonics** moves land masses into cold regions, alters ocean currents, and lifts mountain ranges. Carbon dioxide in air, a cause of **global warming**, is low during cold periods. Lastly, changes in Earth's relation to the Sun occur because of wobbles and variations in the orbit.

RESOURCES

- Bolles, Edmund Blair. *The Ice Finders: How a Poet, a Professor, and a Politician Discovered the Ice Age.* Washington, DC: Counterpoint, 1999.
- Imbrie, John and Katherine Imbrie. *Ice Ages: Solving the Mystery.* Cambridge, MA: Harvard University, 1986.
- MORE ABOUT ICE AGES.
  http://www.museum.state.il.us/exhibits/ice_ages/
  http://oceanworld.tamu.edu/students/iceage/iceage1_sm_table.htm

Immunity

Thucydides (observed immunity effect) ➤ China (administered immunity) ➤ JENNER (smallpox vaccine) ➤ PASTEUR (infectious diseases caused by germs) ➤ PASTEUR/KOCH (bacteria cause disease) ➤ Smith (cholera immunity) ➤ PASTEUR (anthrax immunity) ➤ VON BEHRING/KITASATO (antibodies) ➤ LANDSTEINER (antibodies highly specific) ➤ Discovery of B and T lymphocytes

Immunology—the study of organisms' ability to resist **diseases**—grew from ancient recognition that people who survived certain diseases apparently developed a resist-

ance to further attacks. Thucydides [Greek: died c. 401 B.C.E.], documenting a plague that swept through Athens in 430 B.C.E., observed that individuals who recovered from the plague did not contract it again.

As early as 1000 C.E., the Chinese tried to confer immunity to smallpox by pulverizing and then inhaling the dried skin lesions of smallpox victims. This practice spread through Asia to Europe; while sometimes effective, it also could result in death—and even trigger smallpox epidemics. A major advance occurred in 1796, when **Edward Jenner** developed a cowpox **vaccine** that conferred immunity against smallpox.

FAMOUS FIRST

Antibodies are giant protein molecules. In 1969, Gerald M. Edelman [American: 1929–] created the first precise model of an entire antibody molecule—a 4-chain structure consisting of more than 1,300 amino acids (the building blocks of proteins).

However, immunology as a science did not begin until after 1864, when **Louis Pasteur** established that infectious diseases are caused by germs. After Pasteur and **Robert Koch** proved that some **bacteria** cause disease, researchers identified specific disease agents, which led to development of vaccines and other methods of combating the microorganisms. In 1886, Theobald Smith [American: 1859–1934] showed that the bacteria that cause chicken cholera could confer immunity even after they were killed; Pasteur soon showed that the same was true with anthrax bacteria.

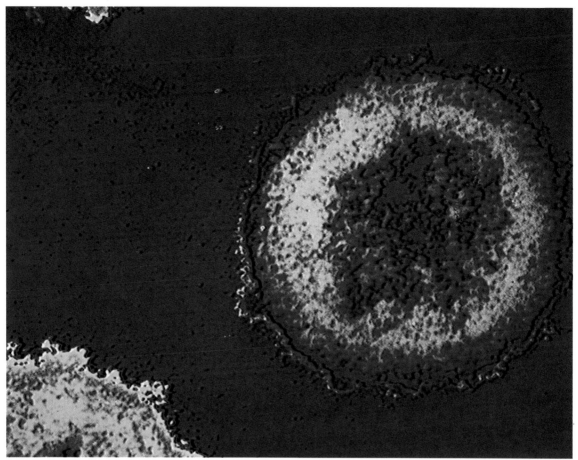

The HIV virus that causes AIDS

The first bacterial toxin to be discovered was that produced by diphtheria bacteria. In 1890, **Emil von Behring** and **Shibasaburo Kitasato** demonstrated that molecules capable of neutralizing this toxin form in the blood of recovering diphtheria patients. They also showed that the molecules—named antibodies—produced by 1 person can neutralize diphtheria toxin in another person. **Karl Landsteiner** discovered that antibodies are highly specific, stimulating interest in the chemistry of immunology.

In the 1940s and 1950s, scientists discovered 2 classes of lymphocytes (a type of white blood cell) called B cells and T cells. B cells were found to be the source of antibodies. T cells regulate the immune response, including activities of B cells.

 RESOURCES

- Cartwright, Frederick F. and Michael Biddiss. *Disease and History*. New York: Sutton, 2000.
- HISTORY OF IMMUNOLOGY.
  http://trevor.butler.edu/jshellha/323/History.html
- LYMPHATIC SYSTEM AND IMMUNITY.
  http://gened.emc.maricopa.edu/bio/bio181/BIOBK/BioBookIMMUN.html

Transportation of goods by railroad helped create the Industrial Revolution.

Industrial Revolution

💡 Transportation by animal power, sailing ships ➤ New manufacture of fibers ➤ Development of steam engine ➤ **KAY** (flying shuttle loom) ➤ **Hargreaves** (spinning jenny) ➤ **Crompton** (spinning mule) ➤ **ARKWRIGHT** (factory spinning machines) ➤ **CARTWRIGHT** (water-powered loom) ➤ **WHITNEY** (cotton gin)

 A revolution is a complete change in a basic way of thinking. During the Industrial Revolution, which occurred from about 1750 to 1900, many people stopped working at home or in small shops and became part of larger enterprises. Wood and stone were often replaced with iron and concrete as building materials. Energy from animals became less important as new ways were found to tap energy from fire and water, then transmit it as electric power. At the beginning of the revolution, transportation was limited to animal power or sailing ships. At the end, much of the world was crossed by railroads, the automobile was becoming popular, and the airplane was just around the corner.

Changes in the manufacture of **fibers** and cloth were an early part of the Industrial Revolution. Before 1750, cloth was made by hand from plants such as flax or from animal hairs, such as wool from sheep. Short pieces of very thin fiber, beaten out of plants or cut from animals, were twisted together to make a single long strand, called yarn. Yarns were woven to make cloth. Although tools such as spin-

Factories line the waterfront.

An illustration shows a nineteenth century steel mill.

ning wheels (for making yarn) and looms (for turning yarn into cloth) were used, each step was done by hand

After 1750, this system changed. The flying shuttle loom, invented by **John Kay** in 1733, produced cloth so fast that yarn became scarce. James Hargreaves [English: 1720–1778] developed a device in 1770 he called the spinning jenny, which could spin 8 times as much yarn as the ordinary spinning wheel. Samuel Crompton [English: 1753– 1827] produced an even better device for making yarn about 1779, the spinning mule. During this period **Richard Arkwright** also invented spinning machines and adapted the machines of others to create the first factory system for making cloth. **Edmund Cartwright**, impressed with Arkwright's system, developed a loom that could run on water power. The invention of the cotton gin by **Eli Whitney** in 1793 helped insure a large supply of cheap cotton.

The **steam engine**, in use from the start of the 1700s, was improved throughout that century. By 1785, steam engines powered a cloth-making factory in England. In the United States, the first steam-powered boat was developed in 1787. In the early 1800s, steamboats and steam-powered railroads became commercial successes. Although most factories continued to use water power because it is inexpensive, movable machinery of all kinds was powered with steam engines.

Steam engines depended on reliable **iron and steel**. Iron became much less expensive after a process for making it with coal instead of wood was introduced in 1735, and even less so after new production methods in 1785. In 1856, new ways to make steel were introduced.

 RESOURCES

- Collins, Mary. *The Industrial Revolution.* Danbury, CT: Children's, 2000. (JUV/YA)
- McCraw, Thomas K. (ed.) *Creating Modern Capitalism: How Entrepreneurs, Companies, and Countries Triumphed in Three Industrial Revolutions.* Cambridge, MA: Harvard University, 1998.
- Pollard, Michael and Philip Wilkinson. *The Industrial Revolution.* Brownall, PA: Chelsea House, 1995. (JUV/YA)
- MORE ABOUT THE INDUSTRIAL REVOLUTION.
  http://137.113.192.101/eprosser/IRlinks.html
  http://www.fordham.edu/halsall/mod/modsbook2.html - indrev

Infrared Radiation

 In 1800, **William Herschel** compared the amount of heat produced by each of the rainbow colors of sunlight passing through a prism. Moving his thermometer outside the bands of light, he observed that invisible radiation below red (Latin "infra" means "below") causes temperature to rise faster than any color of visible sunlight. Herschel had discovered infrared radiation, the part of the electromagnetic spectrum

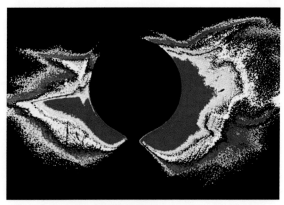

Infrared photograph of the Sun's corona

with waves longer than those of visible light and shorter than microwaves.

The frequency, or number of waves per second, of infrared radiation is in a range that causes most molecules to vibrate faster. But heat is a result of how fast molecules move, so infrared radiation shining on most materials raises their temperature. Similarly, molecular vibration produces infrared radiation, so every physical object radiates some infrared light.

In 1887, William Abney [English: 1843–1920] used chemicals that respond to infrared radiation instead of visible light to make photographs. Conversion of infrared wavelengths to visible light enables night vision based on heat detection, but devices used since World War II by the military to "see" at night instead generate infrared light and then detect its reflection. Some infrared radiation from space passes through the atmosphere and is detected by ground-based telescopes, but, since 1983, space-based telescopes have observed the universe at all infrared wavelengths. Space telescopes, such as *Landsat* I, launched in 1972, also study Earth's infrared radiation, using it to detect differences in vegetation and even mineral deposits.

 **RESOURCES**

• MORE ABOUT INFRARED RADIATION.

http://www.gemini.anu.edu.au/public/
infrared.html

http://www.ipac.caltech.edu/Outreach/Edu/
discovery.html

Ingenhousz, Jan

Physician: discovered photosynthesis
Born: December 8, 1730, Breda, Netherlands
Died: September 7, 1799, Bowood, England

 In the late 1770s, Ingenhousz established the importance of light in plant **physiology**. Based on some 500 experiments, he concluded that during daylight the green parts of plants take in

Jan Ingenhousz discovered photosynthesis in green plants.

carbon dioxide from the air and release oxygen. Darkness stops this process; at night plants—like animals at all times—absorb oxygen and release carbon dioxide.

Ingenhousz had discovered **photosynthesis** (the process by which plants make food), though he did not realize it. But he did appreciate the importance to animals of the gas exchange. By giving off oxygen, he wrote in 1779, plants "have a power to correct bad air, and to improve good air." That is, the release of oxygen by plants makes air fit for animal respiration and, therefore, animal life.

Ingenhousz was an eminent doctor with varied interests. He wrote papers about medicine, electricity, magnetism, and relationships between plants and animals. He invented a machine for generating large amounts of **static electricity** and measured the ability of metal rods to conduct heat.

 **RESOURCES**

• MORE ABOUT JAN INGENHOUSZ.

http://webserver.lemoyne.edu/faculty/
giunta/Ingenhousz.html

http://ftp.bbc.co.uk/history/programmes/
local_heroes/biogs/jingenhousz1.shtml

Interferometer

 Michelson (measured change in speed of light) ➤ **Morley** (further measurement) ➤ **EINSTEIN** (theory of relativity)

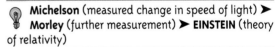 Interferometers are accurate measuring devices based on properties of waves, able to detect movements as slow as 1 inch (2 cm) per 200 years.

The interferometer was invented in 1881 by Albert Michelson [American: 1852–1931] to measure change in the

Albert Michelson

1838–1923] tried again in 1887. The Michelson-Morley experiment also found no effect of Earth's movement. In 1905, **Albert Einstein** used the speed of light as a constant—the same no matter how the measuring device moves, as the Michelson-Morley experiment found—to develop the theory of relativity.

 **RESOURCES**

• SPACE INTERFEROMETRY MISSION.
   http://sim.jpl.nasa.gov/interferometry/

Internal Combustion Engines

Development of steam engines ➤ **Lenoir** (first combustion in cylinder) ➤ **Otto** (improved Lenoir engine; created four-stroke cycle) ➤ **Maybach** (gas powered) ➤ **DIESEL** (diesel engine)

The first devices to convert the energy of burning fuel into motion were **steam engines** that used a separate furnace to turn water into steam, which then moved a rod called a piston in a tube called a cylinder. In 1859, Jean-Joseph-Étienne Lenoir [French: 1822–1900] created the first successful

speed of light caused by Earth's movements through space. Finding none, he developed an even more sensitive interferometer and with Edward Morley [American:

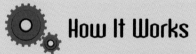 **How It Works**

When superimposed waves have slightly different wavelengths, their peaks sometimes coincide, making higher peaks; but where a peak matches a valley, they cancel. For sound waves, this produces audible beats. Light waves show similar "beats" of brightness and darkness. The same effect occurs for identical waves slightly out of phase. An interferometer uses a mirror to make a wave interfere with its reflection. It is relatively easy to measure distance between beats produced, which is a function of the speed of the original wave.

Most cars use internal combustion engines.

engine to have combustion occur within the cylinder, using expanding gases from burning fuel to move the piston. With coal gas for fuel and a battery to provide the spark, Lenoir's internal combustion engine was much like a modern lawn mower engine that runs on gasoline mixed with lubricating oil. The chief advantage over the steam engine, then and now, of such internal combustion engines is that their size is practical for small appliances, such as powered saws or pumps.

How It Works

In a modern Otto 4-stroke engine, gasoline is mixed with air to form a volatile fuel. A rotating shaft is not only powered by the action of the piston but also moves it into its next position. First, the piston pulls up to draw fuel into the cylinder. Then the piston moves down to compress the fuel. An electric spark from the spark plug ignites the fuel and the resulting explosion produces the power stroke, thrusting the piston up. The piston then moves down to expel the exhaust gases, and the cycle starts again.

In 1867, Nikolaus Otto [German: 1832–1891] improved the Lenoir engine. Like the Lenoir version, Otto's first engine uses an explosion of fuel to lift the piston and, as the lifting gases cool and condense, air pressure pushes the piston back down. The two strokes are uneven, with the noisy piston rising swiftly and falling slowly. By 1877, Otto had found a way to improve engine operation greatly, using 4 strokes instead of 2. The 4-stroke Otto cycle is the basis of large engines that run on gasoline today. The use of gasoline

(instead of a gas) for fuel, however, is based on an 1893 invention of Wilhelm Maybach [German: 1847–1929], whose carburetor vaporizes gasoline and mixes it with air.

Also in 1893, **Rudolf Diesel** developed a different version of ignition for an internal combustion engine. The diesel engine, which can be either 2-stroke or 4-stroke, begins with air alone, which is compressed so much that it becomes hot. Fuel is then injected into the air, so neither spark plug nor carburetor is used.

 RESOURCES

* Heywood, John B. *Internal Combustion Engine Fundamentals*. New York: McGraw-Hill, 1988.
* MORE ABOUT INTERNAL COMBUSTION ENGINES.
  http://home.online.tj.cn/ceze/gasoline.htm

Internet

Licklider (time-sharing, idea of linking information) ➤ **Baran** (transmitting data through network) ➤ Development of interface message processor ➤ Development of ARPANET ➤ **Tomlinson** (e-mail) ➤ Development of personal computers ➤ Development of Internet ➤ **World Wide Web**

 The Internet is a worldwide system of interlinked **computer** networks that allows users to communicate with one another, irrespective of where they are located. Its origins date

Notable Quotable

We techies can look toward the future, envisioning a never-ending stream of wonderful new technologies to help make this world a better place to live.

—Paul Baran

The Internet links computers around the world.

permit scientists at universities and other government contractors to share information. They wanted this network designed in such a way that it would continue to work even if individual computers malfunctioned.

It was decided to develop a distributed network, like the pattern of roads found in a town. If one road is closed, drivers can take an alternate route to their destinations. A distributed computer network similarly is designed with redundant routes. "In parallelism there is strength. Many parts must fail before no path could be found through the network," explained Paul Baran [Polish-American: 1926–]. In 1964, Baran presented an idea for transmitting data through the network. Given the name "packet switching," it was a key element of what would become ARPANET.

In 1969, a new kind of digital switch known as an interface message processor was installed on a computer at the University of California in Los Angeles (UCLA) and on a computer at Stanford Research Institute in Palo Alto, some 400 miles (640 km) to the north. A UCLA

back to time-sharing research begun in the early 1960s. Time-sharing is the simultaneous use of a central computer by two or more people working independently at separate terminals. Among the first to use a time-sharing system was J.C.R. Licklider [American: 1915–1990], who envisioned a system that would be "an Intergalactic Network," linking everyone everywhere to a universe of information. There will come a time, he wrote, when "human brains and computing machines will be coupled."

In 1962, Licklider went to work for the Advanced Research Project Agency (ARPA) of the U.S. Department of Defense. ARPA wanted to create a network that would

Laptop computer with Web page on screen

computer professor and his students proceeded the send the first message to Stanford, and ARPANET was born. Additional computers were added to the network and, in late 1972, it had its first public demonstration at a conference in Washington, D.C.

The next revolutionary step was the invention of e-mail by American engineer Ray Tomlinson. In 1971, Tomlinson was working with an electronic message program called SNDMSG, which he had written to allow people working on the same computer to leave messages for one another in designated "mailboxes." It occurred to him that a program for transferring files among computers could also append material to a mailbox file. He adapted the file transfer program to use SNDMSG to deliver messages to mailboxes on other ARPANET computers. Then he had to find a way to distinguish network messages from those addressed to mailboxes in the local computer. "I used the @ sign to indicate that the user was 'at' some other host rather than being local," he later recalled. Tomlinson's program quickly became a huge success. Within two years, 75% of all ARPANET traffic was e-mail.

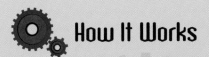

How It Works

Packet switching is a technique that divides a digital message into small units of data called packets. Each packet is coupled with the address of its destination and information on how it is to be reassembled with other packets of data from the same message. The address is read by a routing device at each branch in the network. The routing devices switch the packet on the proper lines until it reaches its destination, where it is combined with the other packets.

Before long, other organizations wanted computer networks. The introduction of personal computers in the late 1970s hastened this trend, and gradually ARPANET evolved into the Internet, accessible by anyone with a computer and a telephone connection. It was the introduction of the

World Wide Web in the early 1990s, however, that rapidly transformed the Internet from a research tool into a consumer and business medium.

RESOURCES

- Hafner, Katie, and Matthew Lyon. *Where Wizards Stay Up Late: The Origins of the Internet.* New York: Simon & Schuster, 1996.
- HISTORY OF THE INTERNET AND WEB.

  http://www.geocities.com/anderberg/ant/history/
- NETIZENS: AN ANTHOLOGY.

  http://www.columbia.edu/rh120/

Iron and Steel

Armenia (fire purifies iron) ➤ China (charcoal and iron ore) ➤ Development of cast iron ➤ **Darby** (method for inexpensive cast iron) ➤ **Development of steel** (wrought iron and carbon) ➤ **Bessemer** (large-scale steel production)

Iron is the second most common metal in Earth's crust but always occurs in combination with other elements. Some metallic iron reaches Earth

Iron tools are strong and tough.

Above: Steel frames make large buildings possible.
Below: A stack of steel girders

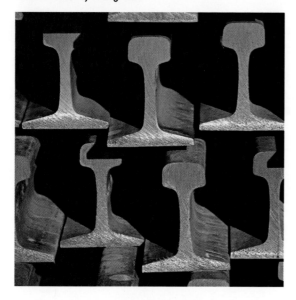

in meteorites, however, and early peoples used meteoric iron to make tools. Around 1500 B.C.E. people in the Armenian mountains learned that very hot fires separate lumps of impure iron from its ore. These lumps can be hammered into weapons and tools. This began the Iron Age, when iron was the dominant material for tools.

Iron produced from lumps separated out in this way is called wrought iron. About 300 B.C.E. the Chinese mixed charcoal with iron ore and burned it in very hot furnaces. In this process some carbon from charcoal dissolves in the iron, lowering the melting point so much that the carbon-iron **alloy** flows as a liquid that can be poured into molds and cast into any shape. Cast iron is not useful for weapons, since it cannot be sharpened, but makes excellent pots. Cast iron—unknown in Europe until the 14th century C.E.—became dominant in the West after Abraham Darby [English: 1677–1717] and sons by 1735 developed a way to make inexpensive cast iron using carbon from coal instead of charcoal.

Steel is a strong, flexible alloy of iron and a small amount of carbon (often with other elements as well). Some steel was made from early times, often by accident. In the West, people learned to add carbon to wrought iron to make small amounts of steel, while in China they reduced the amount of carbon in cast iron by melting it in streams of air. In the 1850s, improved forms of the Chinese method were developed in the United States, England, and Germany—the Bessemer process patented in 1855–1856 by Henry Bessemer [English: 1813–1891] is best known—making steel available in large amounts. Alloys of steel with other metals, such as the stainless steels that do not rust, have been used for special purposes since 1904.

RESOURCES

• MEDIEVAL IRON AND STEEL MANUFACTURE.

http://orb.rhodes.edu/encyclop/culture/scitech/iron_steel.html

Irrigation

  Irrigation is bringing water to land that does not receive enough rainfall to support crops. Farmers have used it since ancient times. Systems of dams that direct river water into canals and ditches, the most common irrigation method, existed in Egypt, the Middle East, and China as early as 5000 B.C.E., near agriculture's start. Irrigation enabled pre-Inca cultures from 1750 B.C.E. to thrive along the Pacific coast of South America.

Many early irrigation systems eventually failed because soil retains minerals, especially salts, as fresh water evaporates from soil surfaces and transpires from crops. Eventually the soil becomes too salty to support most plants and the land and

Irrigation canals

canals are abandoned. Other irrigation networks were destroyed by conquering armies, impoverishing local populations.

Irrigation often requires lifting water to higher levels. An early device for this purpose, still used, is the screw devised by **Archimedes** around 250 B.C.E. From early times, also, water power in the form of water wheels turned by flowing rivers was used to lift water. Pumps based on vacuums were in use in Europe during the Middle Ages to raise water.

Since the beginning of the 20th century, water has been pumped to canals and sprinkler systems, often using hydroelectric power generated at dams to pump water from reservoirs created by those same dams. Giant sprinkler systems, similar to lawn sprinklers, make great green disks that cover arid prairies. Other sprinkler systems automatically move across farm-

land as they spray. Drip irrigation, a water-saving method invented in arid Israel, uses hoses or pipes at ground level or below it to bring water directly to the root systems of crops.

 **RESOURCES**

• National Research Council. *A New Era for Irrigation*. Washington, DC: National Academy, 1998.

Isaacs, Alick

Virologist: discovered interferon
Born: July 17, 1921
Died: January 26, 1967

While studying the influenza virus, Isaacs became interested in the fact that a person who has one viral disease is unlikely to develop another viral disease at the same time. In 1957 he and Swiss

When viruses infect cells, the cells release interferon molecules.

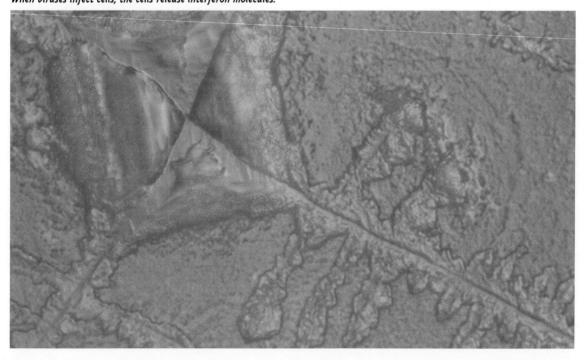

virologist Jean Lindenmann wrote an article that described the virus present in a cell as "interfering" with the activities of a "challenging" virus. They had discovered that inoculating chicken embryo cells with influenza viruses causes the cells to produce a substance they called interferon. The interferon binds to uninfected cells, activating a series of reactions that increase the cells' resistance to attack by both influenza and other viruses. Isaacs and Lindenmann went on to demonstrate that human, monkey, and calf cells also produce interferons.

Interferons have since been shown to be proteins produced by all vertebrate animals, with each species making at least 3 different interferons. Since the 1960s researchers have studied the use of interferons as drugs to treat diseases, and have achieved promising results against illnesses ranging from hepatitis to multiple sclerosis and certain cancers.

See also immunity.

 **RESOURCES**

- HISTORY OF VIROLOGY.

  http://medicine.wustl.edu/virology/timeline.htm

- INTERFERONS.

  http://www.bio.indiana.edu/studies/ugrad/M430/INTERFERON.html

Isotopes

  Unrelated experiments in 1910 showed that the same element can exist in 2 or more forms. The forms, called isotopes of the element, behave the same chemically but differ in mass and degree of **radioactivity**.

In one experiment, **J.J. Thomson** investigated atoms missing one or more electrons. These are moved by electric or magnetic fields at rates based on their mass. Thomson found that neon consists

Each hydrogen isotope has one proton and one electron; the difference is in the number of neutrons.

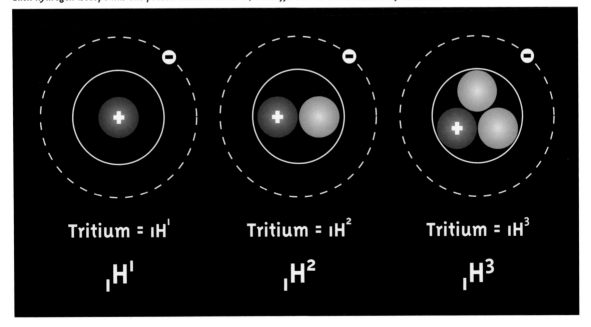

Tritium = $_1H^1$

$_1H^1$

Tritium = $_1H^2$

$_1H^2$

Tritium = $_1H^3$

$_1H^3$

of 2 different types of atoms, 1 with a mass about the same as 20 protons and another with a mass about the same as 22 protons.

YEARBOOK: 1910

- Thomson and Soddy discover isotopes.
- **Thomas Hunt Morgan** learns that some **mutations** are sex-linked.
- **Paul Ehrlich** develops the first chemotherapy.

In the other experiment, Frederick Soddy [English: 1877–1956] observed that a radioactive substance then called "mesothorium" is chemically identical to radium. But "mesothorium" decays into something else at a rate of half a given sample (a half-life) every 6 years, while radium has a half-life of about 1,600 years. Soddy proposed the name isotope (from Greek for "same place") to identify two different elements occupying the same location on the periodic table. "Mesothorium" is now recognized as an isotope of radium rather than a different element.

Isotopes are important in many applications. Slight differences in how organisms metabolize isotopes can be used in dating fossils, identifying temperatures of the past, and determining what early humans ate. Radioactive isotopes trace biological processes, treat cancers, and sterilize foods.

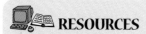 **RESOURCES**

- MORE ABOUT ISOTOPES.
  http://ie.lbl.gov/education/isotopes.htm
  http://www.colorado.edu/physics/2000/isotopes/

Ivanovsky, Dmitri

Microbiologist: discovered viruses
Born: November 9, 1864, Nizy, Russia
Died: June 20, 1920, Rostov-na-Donu, Soviet Union (now Russia)

 "I have found that the sap of leaves attacked by the tobacco mosaic disease retains its infectious qualities even after filtration through Chamberland filtration candles," announced Ivanovsky in 1892. The Chamberland device was a filter with extremely microscopic pores that did not permit passage of bacteria. Therefore, Ivanovsky's "infectious qualities" were smaller than bacteria. He had discovered **viruses** but didn't realize it. Rather, he thought that his filters were defective and that tobacco mosaic disease was caused by bacteria.

Martinus Beijerinck [Dutch: 1851–1931] repeated Ivanovsky's experiments in 1898 and concluded that tobacco mosaic disease is caused by agents he called "filterable viruses" ("virus" is Latin for "poison"). But it wasn't until electron **microscopes** were developed in the 1930s that people first saw the tobacco mosaic viruses.

 RESOURCES

- MORE ABOUT VIRUSES.
  http://www.ucmp.berkeley.edu/alllife/virus.html

Jacquard, Joseph-Marie

Weaver: invented loom that used punched cards
Born: July 7, 1752, Lyon, France
Died: August 7, 1834, Oullins, France

 Some of the earliest factory **automation** began in the **weaving** industry, which Jacquard revolutionized in the early 1800s. Jacquard built the first looms in which a program of instructions automatically controlled the raising of the lengthwise loom threads, called the warp. His concept later was used by **Herman Hollerith** and in **computers**.

Jacquard's program was punched on a series of wooden or paper cards strung together into a kind of tape. Each hole on a card allowed a needle to pass through. The needle was connected by wire to a warp thread. Wherever there were holes on a card, needles would raise warp threads; where there were no holes, the corresponding needles would not pass through and the warp threads would not be raised. As the sequence of cards—one for each row of the carpet or other item being woven—moved through a "reader," the series of instructions produced a specific woven design. After completing a carpet, the cards could be replaced by another set to produce a new carpet with a different design.

Joseph-Marie Jacquard

Loom weaving is faster than hand weaving.

Jacquard's loom wove faster and more accurately than people could weave by hand, which at first caused weavers to fear they would lose their jobs. In Lyon, people destroyed Jacquard's looms and even threatened his life. Nonetheless, Jacquard's idea spread and was soon accepted. By the time of his death more than 30,000 Jacquard looms existed in Lyon alone.

 RESOURCES

• MORE ABOUT JOSEPH-MARIE JACQUARD.
  http://unix1.ccac.edu/tj99/Jacq/
  http://kzoo.edu/k98da01/jloom.html

Jenner, Edward

Physician, naturalist: discovered smallpox vaccination
Born: May 17, 1749, Berkeley, England
Died: January 24, 1823, Berkeley, England

 "If you want to marry a woman who will never be scarred by the 'pox,' marry a milkmaid." This saying was common in rural England in the late 18th century, when smallpox epidemics often raced through communities, killing many and leaving those who recovered covered with ugly scars.

Women who milked cows seldom were smallpox victims. Many had had a related disease, cowpox, which caused only a mild rash of blisters. The cowpox infection seemed to protect against smallpox. If this was true, thought Jenner, could he protect people against smallpox by purposely giving them cowpox?

Edward Jenner

In 1796, a milkmaid with a cowpox blister on her finger visited Jenner. Jenner took some of the fluid from the blister and infected a young boy. The boy developed cowpox and after he recovered Jenner tried to give him smallpox, but the boy did not contract the disease. The cowpox had provided **immunity**.

Jenner called his technique vaccination ("vacca" is Latin for "cow"). The practice quickly spread. Thanks to vaccination, by the beginning of the 21st century smallpox existed only for research purposes, in carefully guarded laboratories. Jenner's work also led to the development of **vaccines** against other diseases.

 RESOURCES

- Jenner, Edward. *Vaccination against Smallpox.* Reprint ed. Amherst, NY: Prometheus, 1996.
- THE EDWARD JENNER MUSEUM.
  http://www.dursley-cotswolds-uk.com/ index.html?/jenner%20museum.html

Jet Engines

WHITTLE (mixed compressed air with fuel for ignition; first test model) ➤ **Ohain** (independently patented same process; first jet engine to fly)

 Jet engines, like **rockets**, work by jet propulsion—a jet of expanded and then ejected gas thrusts the engine forward. About 1928, **Frank Whittle** realized that compressed air from the atmosphere can be mixed with fuel and ignited to form the expanded gases of such a jet. Whittle patented the idea in 1930, but it was not until after World War II started that he got backing to build a jet airplane. Whittle's first test model flew in 1941.

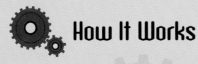

How It Works

Air flowing into a jet engine is compressed by many-bladed fans called rotors. The compressed air mixes with fuel and the mixture explodes. Baffles direct expanding gases backward, turning other rotors that power compression and other operations. The gases are squeezed by a nozzle and flow out the back of the engine in a fluid stream, or jet. The third law of motion requires this backward jet of hot air to produce a forward force on the engine.

In 1933, Hans von Ohain [German: 1911–1998] independently had the same idea as Whittle, which von Ohain discovered when he patented his own, slightly different version. But von Ohain's engine was the first to fly, on August 27, 1939. Near the end of World War II, jet-propelled aircraft participated in battles on both sides.

Jet engine

Jets entered commercial aviation in 1952, but did not become successful until after 1958. Today, nearly all commercial and military aircraft are jets.

 RESOURCES

• Gunston, Bill. *The Development of Jet and Turbine Aero Engines.* 2nd ed. Sparkford, Somerset, UK: Haynes, 1998.

• Hunecke, Klaus. *Jet Engines: Fundamentals of Theory, Design, and Operation.* Osceola, WI: Motorbooks International, 1998.

• MORE ABOUT JET ENGINES.

http://school.discovery.com/homeworkhelp/worldbook/atozscience/j/288060.html

Joliot-Curie, Irène & Frédéric

Physicists: discovered artificial radioactivity
Irène: **Born:** September 12, 1897, Paris, France
Died: March 17, 1956, Paris, France
Frédéric: Born: March 19, 1900, Paris, France
Died: August 14, 1958, Paris, France

 When he went to work for Pierre and **Marie Curie** in 1925, Frédéric Joliot met their elder daughter, Irène, who introduced him to the study of **radioactivity**. When Frédéric and Irène married in 1926, they combined their last names.

In 1930, the Joliot-Curies developed a way to produce very energetic alpha particles (helium nuclei) using polonium, the first radioactive element discovered by Irène's parents. The Joliot-Curies began bombarding various elements with alpha particles. In 1933, they found that when aluminum is bombarded, some alpha particles are absorbed by the aluminum atoms, changing them to radioactive phosphorus atoms. These atoms are **isotopes** of— different versions of—naturally occurring phosphorus atoms. The Joliot-Curies had discovered

The Joliot-Curies: Frédéric (above) and Irène (below)

artificial radioactivity. Using the same technique they went on to produce radioactive forms of additional elements that normally are not radioactive. Today, radioactive isotopes are important in **medical imaging** and cancer treatments.

NOBEL PRIZE 1935

The Joliet-Curies received the Nobel Prize in chemistry "in recognition of their synthesis of new radioactive elements."

In 1938, the Joliot-Curies repeated German experiments in bombarding uranium, a naturally occurring radioactive element, with **subatomic particles** called neutrons. They found an element with atoms smaller than uranium atoms in the product. The work led to the recognition by **Lise Meitner** of atomic fission and eventually to creation of the atomic bomb.

 RESOURCES

• BIOGRAPHY OF IRÈNE JOLIOT-CURIE.

 http://www.nobel.se/chemistry/laureates/1935/joliot-curie-bio.html

• BIOGRAPHY OF JEAN FRÉDÉRIC JOLIOT.

 http://www.nobel.se/chemistry/laureates/1935/joliot-bio.html

Julian, Percy Lavon

Chemist: synthesized organic chemicals
Born: April 11, 1899, Montgomery, Alabama
Died: April 19, 1975, Chicago, Illinois

  Julian gained fame for synthesizing several compounds of medical importance. His first

Percy Lavon Julian

Sweet potatoes

important contribution came in 1935 while investigating plants used in traditional medicines. From the calabar bean he synthesized physostigmine, a drug used to treat glaucoma (an eye disease that can result in blindness).

Later on, Julian synthesized the female hormone progesterone and the male hormone testosterone using compounds extracted from soybean oil. He also made

synthetic cortisone from a wild species of sweet potato. His product was much less expensive but just as effective as natural cortisone, which had been shown to be useful in treating rheumatoid arthritis and other inflammatory conditions.

Julian also invented a commercial process for preparing soybean protein, which could be used to coat and size paper and textiles, and to create cold-water paints. During World War II, he used soybean protein to develop AeroFoam, a substance that extinguishes oil and gasoline fires.

 RESOURCES

• MORE ABOUT PERCY LAVON JULIAN.

http://www.pbs.org/wgbh/aso/databank/entries/bmjuli.html

http://www.invent.org/book/book-text/60.html

YEARBOOK: 1956

• Julian's method of preparing cortisone is patented.
• **Arthur Kornberg** synthesizes **DNA**.
• **Dorothy Crowfoot Hodgkin** determines the structure of vitamin B12.

Kamerlingh Onnes, Heike

Physicist: discovered superconductivity
Born: September 21, 1853, Groningen, The Netherlands
Died: February 21, 1926, Leyden, The Netherlands

 Kamerlingh Onnes, a pioneer in the field of low-temperature physics, spent his career attaining and study-

Notable Quotable

I should like to write "through measuring is knowing" as a motto above each physics laboratory.

—Heike Kamerlingh Onnes

ing the effects of temperatures approaching absolute zero (0 K or -273.15° C). His first major achievement came in 1908, when he became the first scientist to liquefy the gas helium, at 4.2 K (-269° C).

NOBEL PRIZE 1913

Kamerlingh Onnes received the Nobel Prize in physics "for his investigations on the properties of matter at low temperatures which led, inter alia, to the production of liquid helium."

Heike Kamerlingh Onnes

Kamerlingh Onnes also studied the ability of metals to conduct electricity at very low temperatures. In 1911 he froze mercury and measured its resistance to the passage of electricity. The lower the temperature, the less the resistance. For example, at 10 K the electrical resistance was 1/100th of what it was at room temperature. When he lowered the temperature to 4.2 K, something unexpected happened: all electrical resistance disappeared and electric current flowed continually through the solid mercury. Kamerlingh Onnes had discovered a phenomenon he called **superconductivity**. He tested numerous additional metals and found that certain of them also exhibited superconductivity at low temperatures.

FAMOUS FIRST

Working in the Kamerlingh Onnes laboratory in 1926, Willem Hendrik Keesom [Dutch: 1876–1956] became the first person to solidify helium.

 RESOURCES

- BIOGRAPHY OF HEIKE KAMERLINGH ONNES.

  http://www.nobel.se/physics/laureates/1913/onnes-bio.html

- SUPERFLUID HELIUM.

  http://chemistry.about.com/science/chemistry/library/weekly/aa052900a.htm?iam=dpile&terms=%2BKamerlingh+%2BOnnes+%2Bsuperconductivity

Kay, John

Inventor: developed the flying shuttle for weaving
Born: July 16, 1704, near Bury, England
Died: c. 1780, France

 Until the 1730s, loom **weaving** was a slow, tedious process. The shuttle bearing the yarn had to be passed from one side of the loom to the other by hand. To make wide fabrics, two workers were needed to pass the shuttle across the loom.

In 1733, Kay patented a new type of shuttle. A grooved "race board" ran horizontally across the loom, with a shuttle box at each end. When a worker pulled a cord attached to the shuttle, the shuttle would "fly" across the race board. A single worker could weave fabrics of better quality and any width faster than two workers could before.

Kay's invention dramatically changed the weaving industry and was an important step toward the **Industrial Revolution**. Though textile manufacturers adopted Kay's invention, they avoided paying royalties and Kay lost most of his money trying to defend his patent. Then in 1753 a mob of workers, fearing the flying shuttle would cause unemployment, ransacked Kay's home. Kay fled to France, where he is believed to have died in poverty.

 **RESOURCES**

- The "Flying Shuttle."
  http://www.saburchill.com/history/chapters/IR/009.html
- The Industrial Revolution.
  http://www.eurohist.com/the_industrial_revolution.htm

Kekulé, Friedrich

Chemist: pioneered organic chemistry
Born: September 7, 1829, Darmstadt, Germany
Died: July 13, 1896, Bonn, Germany

 Kekulé was a young architecture student when the burned body of a neighbor was found. People believed she had drunk enough alcohol to make her flammable. At a trial in 1850, the noted chemist Justus von Liebig [German: 1803–1873] testified that the woman would have died long before she could have drunk so much alcohol. Then Kekulé described an unusual ring worn by the woman, on which were carved two snakes, each biting the other's tail. The ring was found in the possession of a servant, who was convicted of murder based on the tes-

Friedrich Kekulé

timony of Liebig and Kekulé. Kekulé was so impressed by Liebig that he decided to study chemistry with him. Perhaps it was his early interest in architecture that led him to focus on the chemical structure of **molecules**.

In 1858, Kekulé presented two basic principles of organic chemistry (the chemistry of carbon compounds). First, he said that carbon has a valence of 4; that is, in a stable compound each carbon atom forms 4 bonds with other atoms. Second, he said that carbon atoms can form chains by linking with one another.

Several years later Kekulé was trying to determine the arrangement of the 6 carbon atoms in a benzene molecule. One day he fell asleep while thinking of this problem and dreamed of the murdered woman's ring. Kekulé realized that the carbon atoms in the benzene molecule could be like the two snakes, forming a circle, or hexagonal ring.

 **RESOURCES**

• Kekulé and Carbon.
   http://bogle.chem.wsu.edu/phs298/Kekule.html

Kelvin, William Thomson, Baron

Physicist: introduced idea of absolute zero
Born: June 26, 1824, Belfast, Ireland (now Northern Ireland)
Died: December 17, 1907, Netherhall, Scotland

 In 1892, William Thomson was honored for his work by being named Baron Kelvin of Largs; today he generally is known as Kelvin. His many contributions included the concept of a temperature scale that begins at absolute zero—the temperature at which objects contain absolutely no **heat** energy. Absolute zero, or zero kelvin (0 K), is -469.67° F (-273.15° C). Above this point every 1 K equals 1° C.

In 1849, Thomson coined the word "thermodynamics" for the young science that studies heat movement and the conversion of heat to useful work. He was one of the first people to formulate the second law of thermodynamics, which says that in a closed system heat flows from a hot region to a cooler region. To reverse the process, as in a refrigerator, energy must be added to the system.

In experiments with James Prescott Joule [English: 1818–1889], Kelvin proved that gases cool as they expand —an idea today known as the Joule–Thomson effect.

Baron William Thomson Kelvin

In 1854, Thomson switched his attention to the possibility of laying an underwater telegraph cable across the Atlantic. He became rich when he designed a **telegraph** receiver, called a mirror galvanometer, for use on the cable, which was successfully laid in 1858. He

YEARBOOK: 1873

- Thomson invents a device for predicting tides.
- Charles Wyville Thomson [Scottish: 1830–1882], leader of the *Challenger* expedition, finds manganese nodules on the floor of the Atlantic.
- **Heinrich Schliemann** discovers ancient Troy.
- **Camillo Golgi** develops a new way to stain cells.

also invented a compass, a device for measuring tides and calculating tide tables, and other devices.

RESOURCES

- Burchfield, Joe D. *Lord Kelvin and the Age of the Earth.* Chicago: University of Chicago, 1990.
- Hoskin, Michael A. (ed.) *The Cambridge Illustrated History of Astronomy.* New York: Cambridge University, 1997.

Kepler, Johannes

Astronomer: discovered laws governing orbits of planets
Born: December 27, 1571, Weil der Stadt, Germany
Died: November 15, 1630, Regensburg, Germany

"Just as the eye was made to see colors, and the ear to hear sounds, so the human mind was made to understand, not whatever you please, but quantity," wrote Kepler. A giant of the **Scientific Revolution**, he based his investigations on careful observations and complex mathematics.

Kepler built on the work of **Tycho Brahe** and **Nicolaus Copernicus** to discover the three mathematical laws that describe a planet's orbit, the speed at which it travels, and the time it needs to complete a revolution around the Sun. He proved that Earth and other planets travel in orbits that are ellipses, not circles as had been believed since ancient times. And he showed that the speed of a planet in its orbit is not uniform, but decreases as its distance from the Sun increases, thus overthrowing another long-held belief.

Kepler also was a founder of the modern science of optics. He was the first to correctly explain how people see—he noted that the pupil of the eye functions as a diaphragm and that light rays are focused on the retina.

Johannes Kepler

FAMOUS FIRST

In 1619, Kepler explained how a **comet** gets its tail. He said that emissions from the Sun—today called the solar wind—push material out of the comet's head into a long tail that points away from the Sun.

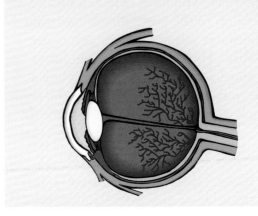

He also explained why eyeglasses help people see better. After **Galileo** sent him one of the first telescopes, he explained how the instrument works and improved its design.

Above: *The human eye*
Below: *The solar system*

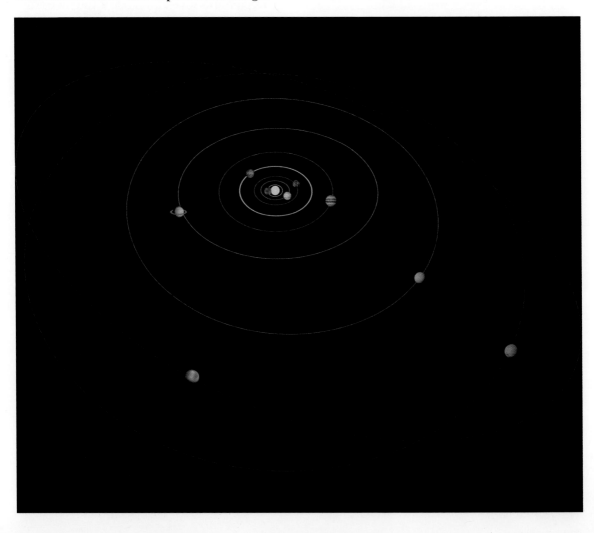

RESOURCES

- Caspar, Max. *Kepler*. Mineola, NY: Dover, 1993.
- Voelkel, James R. *Johannes Kepler: And the New Astronomy*. New York: Oxford University, 1999. (JUV/YA)
- MORE ABOUT JOHANNES KEPLER.

  http://www-groups.dcs.st-and.ac.uk/history/Mathematicians/Kepler.html

  http://es.rice.edu/ES/humsoc/Galileo/People/kepler.html

Kettering, Charles

Engineer: invented the electric starter
Born: August 29, 1876, Loudonville, Ohio
Died: November 25, 1958, Dayton, Ohio

 At the beginning of the 1900s, starting an **automobile** involved turning a hand crank located at the front of the car. Sometimes a car jumped into gear when it started up, or the engine backfired, injuring or even killing the person doing the cranking

YEARBOOK: 1912

- The Cadillac is the first car to feature a self-starter.
- An American doctor invents the heating pad.
- A Swiss company builds the first diesel locomotive.

Charles Kettering invented a motor started by turning a key.

(usually the owner, since each car had peculiarities unfamiliar to anyone else). As soon as the engine fired, the person had to rush to the driver's seat to advance the spark and retard the throttle. Otherwise, the engine quit and the process had to be repeated.

"More than once, we have seen research accomplishments fit together, like the words of a crossword puzzle, to aid us in solving other problems," recalled Kettering. Soon after graduating from college he had invented the electric cash register. When a button was pushed, a small motor generated a burst of power to open the register's drawer. Based on this invention Kettering created the self-starting motor for automobiles. It runs off a storage battery and is today operated by turning a key.

Kettering also invented engines and improved lighting and ignition systems. He contributed to the development of fuels, shock absorbers, fast-drying lacquer paints, and 4-wheel brakes.

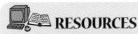

RESOURCES

- THE INVENTIONS OF CHARLES KETTERING.

   http://www.vintagecars.about.com/autos/
   vintagecars/library/weekly/aao82998.htm

Khorana, Har Gobind

Geneticist: helped crack genetic code
Born: January 9, 1922, Raipur, India (now in Pakistan)

There are two "alphabets" in a cell. One consists of the 4 different kinds of nucleotide bases that are found in **DNA** molecules. The second consists of 20

Har Gobind Khorana

NOBEL PRIZE 1968

Khorana shared the Nobel Prize for physiology or medicine with Nirenberg and Robert W. Holley [American: 1922–] for cracking the genetic code.

different amino acids, the building blocks of proteins. How does the first alphabet form a code that translates into the second alphabet?

In the 1960s, building on work by **Marshall W. Nirenberg** and others, Khorana proved that the genetic code is spelled in 3-letter combinations, or "words," called codons. He synthesized all of the 64 possible 3-letter words made from 4 nucleotides. In some cases, several words ("synonyms") code for the same amino acid. Khorana learned that other words ("punctuation marks") signal the cell to start or stop making proteins.

FAMOUS FIRST

In 1970, Khorana made the first completely artificial **gene**, a copy of a yeast gene.

Khorana was the first scientist to synthesize strings of nucleotides, called oligonucleotides. Today, custom-designed oligonucleotides have a wide range of applications in **cloning** and **genetic engineering**.

RESOURCES

- MORE ABOUT HAR GOBIND KHORANA.

   http://www.nobel.se/medicine/laureates/
   1968/khorana-bio.html

   http://www.nobel.se/medicine/laureates/
   1968/index.html

Kipping, Frederick Stanley

Chemist: discovered silicone plastics
Born: August 16, 1863, Manchester, England
Died: May 1, 1949, Criccieth, Wales

 Silicones are among today's most widely used **plastics**. Because of their exceptional resistance to water and temperature extremes, silicones are used as water repellents, sealants, adhesives, lubricants, synthetic rubber, and insulation.

Silicones are polymers—very long molecules composed of repeating units. The "backbone" of each silicone molecule consists of alternating silicon and oxygen atoms. They were first created by Kipping around 1900, and he spent 40 years making and investigating the compounds. But he thought his "gluelike" silicones were unimportant and unlikely to be of any value.

Then around 1940, Eugene G. Rochow [American: 1909–] discovered the excellent insulating properties of methyl silicone and also developed a practical, low-cost process for synthesizing silicones. Commercial production of silicones began several years later.

 RESOURCES

• A CONCISE HISTORY OF PLASTICS.
  http://www.nswpmitb.com.au/
  HistoryOfPlastics.html

Silicone plastics are used in many ways, including syringes, lipstick, pacifiers, and tubing.

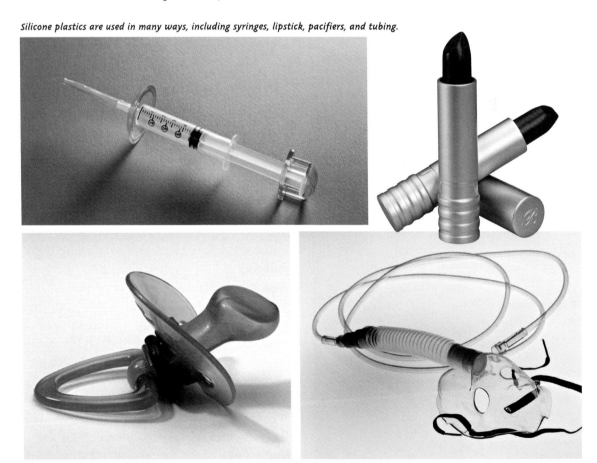

Kirchoff, Gustav Robert

Physicist: founded spectrum analysis
Born: March 12, 1824, Königsberg, Prussia (now Kaliningrad, Russia)
Died: October 17, 1887, Berlin, Germany

  Kirchhoff's major achievements were in spectrum analysis (using **spectrocopes** to study the spectrum of light given off by an object). He and Robert W. Bunsen [German: 1811–1899] founded this science in the 1850s. They showed that when an element is heated, it emits a colored light that can be separated by a prism into a spectrum (range pattern) of wavelengths. Each element's spectrum of wavelengths is unique—for example, that of iron is differ-

Robert Gustav Kirchoff

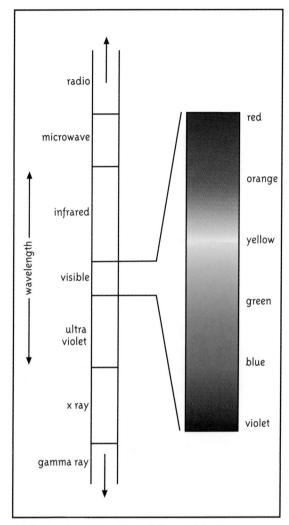

Kirchoff's experiments separated elements into spectrums.

ent from that of aluminum. Applying their technique, Kirchhoff and Bunsen discovered two previously unknown elements, cesium and rubidium.

Kirchhoff then used spectrum analysis to study the composition of the Sun, thereby expanding chemical research beyond Earth and opening a new era in astronomy. He explained that the many dark lines in the Sun's spectrum represent wavelengths of light absorbed by various elements in the Sun's atmosphere.

Earlier in his career Kirchhoff built on work by Georg Simon Ohm [German: 1789–1854], who explained that electric current decreases as resistance of the conductor increases. Kirchhoff devised laws that allow calculation of the currents, voltages, and resistances of electrical circuits. He also demonstrated that current flows through a conductor at the speed of light.

 **RESOURCES**

• GUSTAV KIRCHHOFF (1824–1887).
   http://www.hao.ucar.edu/public/education/sp
   /images/kirchhoff.html

Kitasato, Shibasaburo

Bacteriologist: co-discovered a type of immunity
Born: December 20, 1852, Kumamoto, Japan
Died: June 13, 1931, Nakanocho, Japan

 Kitasato worked in the laboratory of **Robert Koch** from 1885 to 1891. In 1889 he became the first person to obtain a pure culture of tetanus bacteria. Then he and a colleague, **Emil von Behring**, demonstrated that giving healthy animals small doses of blood from an animal infected with tetanus produces **immunity** in the healthy animals. They similarly showed that doses of sterilized diphtheria bacteria produce immunity to diphtheria in humans.

Kitasato returned to Japan in 1892, where he established a laboratory to study infectious diseases. In 1894, an outbreak of bubonic plague occurred in Hong Kong, drawing Kitasato and other scientists eager to unravel the mystery of how this ancient disease is transmitted. Within weeks of their arrival Kitasato and Alexandre Yersin [French:

Shibasaburo Kitasato

1863–1943] independently discovered the infectious agent of bubonic plague, the bacterium *Yersinia pestis*.

 RESOURCES

• HISTORY OF IMMUNOLOGY.
   http://trevor.butler.edu/jshellha/323/
   History.html

Kites

Asia (first kites) ➤ **Europe** (first scientific use) ➤ **FRANKLIN** (used to study lightning) ➤ **WRIGHT BROTHERS** (used kites to develop airplane) ➤ Hargrave (box kite) ➤ **Rogallo** (frameless kite, hang glider)

  The first kites were made in eastern Asia at least 2,000 years ago; kites have been

Above: *Kite with long tail*
Left: *Children launching a kite*

popular in China, Japan, India, and Malaysia ever since, and in other parts of the world more recently. Europeans first learned of Asian kites from the writings of Marco Polo in 1298. Europeans were themselves flying kites by the early 1400s.

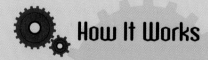 **How It Works**

A kite uses energy of moving air to rise into the sky. A line, called a tether, controls the relationship of the kite to the wind. The simplest kite is a sail held open with a frame, a tail hanging down to stabilize it, and a tether attached to the midpoint for control.

Kites were used to lift people and objects off the ground before balloons or airplanes had been invented. The first scientific use of a kite to study weather conditions high above the ground was in 1749 and meteorologists continued the practice until the 1930s, when aircraft and reliable **balloons** became available. **Benjamin Franklin** used a kite to study lightning. During World War I (1914–18) German **submarines** pulled kites to lift observers. Kites also have provided observation platforms for cameras and created radio antennas for lifeboats.

Many inventors, including the **Wright brothers**, used kites to help understand how to lift and control **airplanes**. One, Lawrence Hargrave [Australian: 1850–1915], developed the box kite in 1893. Hargrave also created kites that were curved like the wings of a modern airplane.

A frameless kite strong enough to carry a person was invented by Francis Rogallo [American: 1912–] and his wife Gertrude in 1948. A free-flying Rogallo kite steered by its rider is called a hang **glider**.

A Rogallo kite is also known as a hang glider.

RESOURCES

- Eden, Maxwell. *The Magnificent Book of Kites: Explorations in Design, Construction, Enjoyment and Flight*. New York: Black Dog & Leventhal, 1998.
- Pelham, David. *Kites*. New York: Overlook, 2000.
- MORE ABOUT KITES.

  http://www.aka.org.au/
  kites_in_the_classroom/history.htm

  http://www.sound.net/kiteguy/japkites.html

  http://www.kites.org/

  http://www.asahi-net.or.jp/et3m-tkkw/
  history-table.html

Koch, Robert

Bacteriologist: proved some bacteria cause disease
Born: December 11, 1843, Clausthal, Germany
Died: May 27, 1910, Baden-Baden, Germany

 Koch helped found bacteriology—the science of **bacteria**. In 1876 he devised a procedure to demonstrate that the bacterium **Bacillus anthracis** causes anthrax, a disease of animals. It was the first time that a particular bacterium was shown to be the cause of a particular disease.

Koch's procedure is still used today to prove that a specific organism is the cause

A petri dish is used for growing bacteria cultures.

Robert Koch

of a specific disease. It consists of 4 steps called Koch's Postulates. First, the organism suspected of causing the disease must be found in the sick host and isolated from it. Second, the organism must be grown in pure cultures in the laboratory. Third, a healthy host must be inoculated with the organism and must become sick with the disease. Fourth, the organism must be isolated from the new host.

NOBEL PRIZE 1905

Koch received the Nobel Prize in physiology or medicine "for his investigations and discoveries in relation to tuberculosis."

Koch also identified the microorganisms that cause tuberculosis, amoebic dysentery, cholera, and other diseases. His laboratory attracted many bright pupils, who also made major discoveries.

"I have undertaken my investigations in the interests of public health and I hope the greatest benefits will accrue therefrom," he wrote. It was a goal he achieved.

 **RESOURCES**

* Biography of Robert Koch.

    http://www.nobel.se/medicine/laureates/1905/koch-bio.html

* Microbiology.

    http://www-micro.msb.le.ac.uk/109/History.html

Kornberg, Arthur

Biochemist: synthesized DNA
Born: March 3, 1918, Brooklyn, New York

 "Without knowing and respecting **enzymes**, better still loving them, answers to the most basic questions of growth, development, and disease will remain beyond reach," believes Kornberg. His work on the biochemistry of enzymes and coenzymes (proteins that assist enzymes) led to his synthesis of **DNA** molecules.

In the mid-1950s researchers were eager to learn how DNA makes copies of itself. **James D. Watson** and **Francis Crick**

NOBEL PRIZE 1959

Kornberg shared the Nobel Prize in physiology or medicine with Severo Ochoa [Spanish: 1905–1993], who synthesized RNA (ribonucleic acid).

Arthur Kornberg

suggested that each DNA molecule contains all the information needed for replication. This was proved to be true by Kornberg in 1956, when he discovered an enzyme called DNA polymerase. He placed in a test tube the enzyme, some DNA, and the 4 types of nucleotides that are the building

Notable Quotable

In research, it is up to me to select a corner of the giant jigsaw puzzle of nature and then find and fit a missing piece. When after false starts and fumbling, a piece falls into place and provides clues for more, I take pleasure in having done something creative.

—Arthur Kornberg

blocks of DNA. The enzyme organized in sequence the nucleotides to assemble an exact copy of the DNA. It was the first time that DNA had been synthesized. Since then, researchers around the world have used DNA polymerase to make and study DNA.

RESOURCES

• More about Arthur Kornberg.

http://www.thescientist.com/yr1989/sep/opin_890904.html

http://www.nobel.se/medicine/laureates/1959/kornberg-bio.html

Krebs, Hans Adolf

Biochemist: discovered the citric acid cycle
Born: August 25, 1900, Hildesheim, Germany
Died: November 22, 1981, Oxford, England

 An essential part of **metabolism** is the production of energy. Most organisms obtain the energy they need from the oxidation of food. During oxidation, large food molecules are broken down into carbon dioxide and water molecules and energy is released. In the 1930s, Krebs identified a complex series of chemical changes involved in converting food into energy. This pathway is now called the citric acid cycle or Krebs cycle.

Krebs discovered that during the cycle citric acid is repeatedly formed and broken

Hans Adolf Krebs

down. The citric acid molecule is built around a chain of 6 carbon atoms. After several steps in the cycle this becomes shortened to a 5-carbon compound, which is changed to a 4-carbon compound. Eventually, a 4-carbon compound picks up a 2-carbon compound to once again form citric acid. During the process, energy in the form of molecules of ATP (adenosine triphosphate) is released. The ATP can then be used to power various reactions in cells.

NOBEL PRIZE 1953

The Nobel Prize in physiology or medicine was awarded to Krebs, for discovery of the citric acid cycle, and Fritz Albert Lipmann [German-American: 1899–1986], for discovery of co-enzyme A and its importance in metabolism.

 ### RESOURCES

• Biography of Sir Hans Adolf Krebs.

http://www.nobel.se/medicine/laureates/1953/krebs-bio.html